# Crossings

## H. K. JEJI

# Foliohut Press LLC

Questions can be addressed through the website:
www.foliohutpress.com
Published by Foliohut Press LLC.

ISBN: 0991396804
EAN: 9780991396801
Library of Congress Control Number: 2013956215
Foliohut Press

*To my Prajna*

# CHARACTERS

*A few days in the lives of Indian immigrants living in North America during the first decade of the 2000s.*

---

**CHACHA JI.** He has short hair and a beard. He is well dressed but casual. He has an upbeat personality and an ease of manners.

**PREET.** Chacha ji's daughter.

**BACHAN.** He has short hair and is casually dressed. He has easy but restrained mannerisms.

**NIRMAL.** Bachan's wife.

**ROOP.** Bachan's son.

**THE CAPTAIN.** He is physically fit and well dressed in a turban and a tie. His mannerisms are controlled and disciplined.

**NEELUM.** The Captain's wife. She has a sophisticated look.

NEETU. The Captain's daughter. There is an air of youthfulness and openness about her. Her long hair is stylishly done and hangs over her shoulders.

*It is understood that all of the characters except ROOP are first generation immigrants; therefore, the actors' use of English spoken with an Indian accent is encouraged.

**PREET and NEETU can be played by the same actor, and similarly, CHACHA JI and THE CAPTAIN can be played by the same actor.

*** The parents are in their fifties and their children are in their twenties.

# SCENE ONE

*The family room has a television set, cordless phone, and modern furniture. It is decorated with Punjabi artifacts and wall hangings. The desk and desktop computer are situated in such a way that a user can converse easily with others in the room.*

*Late Saturday morning.*

*Nirmal is dressed for company, and she has on an apron. The living room is in disarray; the silver, china, and other odds and ends are lying all over. Nirmal is busy tidying up and dusting around the room, and Bachan has just finished vacuuming. The vacuum cleaner cord is still in the socket. Amid all the commotion, Bachan sits silently on the sofa, engrossed in reading his newspaper.*

---

NIRMAL: You must be serious once in a while. It is a serious business.

BACHAN: You are making it a business. It does not have to be.

NIRMAL: The family is used to being waited upon hand and foot. You know how military families are back home.

BACHAN: We are not back home.

NIRMAL (*tensely*): Would it be so wrong, just once in your life, just once to go along?

BACHAN (*smiling*): Don't I do that every day?

NIRMAL: That will be the day! Now, make sure you have the drinks ready. The Captain is very particular about his drinks. After dinner, make sure you lead them to the living room. Don't slide into the family room as you usually do with your friends. And one more thing, do make an effort to carry on the conversation. Don't leave everything up to me.

BACHAN (*lightly*): But you carry on very well on your own. You rarely need my help there. You get along with Neelum…the Captain, and I don't have to say a word.

NIRMAL: Oh, be serious. You need to say something. Ask something.

BACHAN (*baffled*): Ask something? What do you mean? I am not interested in asking anything, or knowing anything about them. If they want to tell me, it's their business.

NIRMAL (*annoyed*): You are marrying your son into that family, and you do not plan to ask anything?

BACHAN (*incredulously*): Now let us be clear. You want to marry your son into that family. You are the one putting on this monkey show. Their daughter is coming in this house. My son is not going to their house. They should be asking us the questions. And asking questions? What a rubbish idea. Do you think they will come out and tell me that their daughter has robbed a bank? Or that she lies, or spends money as if there is no end to it, or that she does not know how to boil water—

NIRMAL (*annoyed, raising her voice*): Yes, yes, I understand. You don't have to question them, but don't sit like a statue as you usually do when things don't go your way.

BACHAN: You assume too many things about me. I am not against this as long as it is what our son wants.

NIRMAL: They have to like our family too.

BACHAN: What is there not to like? We are God-fearing, hardworking people. So is our son. He is a good boy. What else could they want?

NIRMAL: You know how things are these days.

BACHAN: No, I don't know how things are these days. Are they any different from when we got married?

NIRMAL: Why do you have to be so difficult all the time?

BACHAN (*smiling*): I am the easiest person to get along with.

NIRMAL: You need to wake up to the realities of this world.

BACHAN: What are those realities? You have to tell me. Do not go around in circles.

NIRMAL (*resignedly*): Sometimes, you can be so difficult.

BACHAN (*decisively*): I get tired of listening to this, me being difficult and all that sort of thing. Why don't you tell me where to sit, where to stand, give me a script to memorize, and I will follow it to the last detail? Don't go in circles. I will do exactly as you wish.

NIRMAL: Oh hush! You never listen.

BACHAN (*baffled*): That's all I have been doing, listening. Please do explain yourself. I don't want to be blamed for the failure of this project of yours.

NIRMAL (*annoyed*): Project? Failure? For you, it is a project? You are just impossible!

BACHAN: Now, don't get yourself worked up. Everything will work out.

NIRMAL: The only thing I am asking for is a little support.

BACHAN: A little support! But you have my full support.

NIRMAL: You swear you won't do anything to ruin it for me, for our son?

BACHAN (*tenderly*): Now, you've hurt my feelings. Why would I do that?

NIRMAL: When the caterers come, will you make sure everything is taken care of? On the dining table there is a list of things they are supposed to bring.

BACHAN: Now, that I will do.

NIRMAL: And then get ready. (*Bachan exits. Raising her voice*) Roop, *beta[1]*, come here.

(*Roop enters.*)

ROOP: Yes, Mom?

---

1 *beta.* Son

NIRMAL: Would you please vacuum the basement and stairs, and then get ready? Please don't wear jeans.

ROOP: But, Mom.

NIRMAL: Please.

ROOP: Yes, Mom.

NIRMAL: And be on your best behavior.

ROOP: Yes, Mom.

(*Bachan returns with a tray of tea mugs and snacks and places it on the coffee table.*)

BACHAN: Take a break. I made tea for us.

(*Nirmal removes her apron and sits beside Roop.*)

NIRMAL (*to Roop*): Keep an eye on your father as well.

ROOP (*looking at Bachan with a smile*): Yes, Mother.

NIRMAL: It is a good family, a well-to-do family. I saw the girl the other day. She is a very charming young lady. You will like her right away. I am sure of that.

ROOP: Mother, have you known the girl for a long time?

NIRMAL: Well, I know her mother from our college days. Then she married that military man. They are a well-traveled and educated family. Every two or three years, they were stationed in a different place. They have seen the entire country.

BACHAN (*sardonically*): And here you are, stuck with a factory worker!

NIRMAL: Did I ever complain?

BACHAN: You would have been better-off marrying an officer.

NIRMAL (*resignedly*): Why don't you let me ever speak well about other people? It does not mean that I am unhappy. I am very happy with my life.

ROOP (*to Nirmal*): Mom, when did you meet the girl?

NIRMAL: Last summer, when I went to Vancouver to see your aunt.

ROOP (*surprised*): You have only met her once?

NIRMAL: And I went to see them last week. They are visiting their relatives here.

ROOP: So, you have only seen her twice!

NIRMAL (*troubled*): Where are you going with all this?

ROOP: I just want to know how well you know her.

NIRMAL: She is a very polite, sweet girl. You will like her.

ROOP: You shouldn't get upset if things don't work out. You promised that you would not force me. And she may not even like me. Who knows? Just take it easy.

NIRMAL (*insistently*): You should tell me right now if there is another girl.

ROOP: No, Mom, I swear. At this time, I don't, but I don't think this is the girl. You yourself have met her only twice.

NIRMAL: You will like her. I promise.

ROOP: I know girls in college whom I like, but I don't want to marry them. It has to be more than liking.

NIRMAL: I promise. She is a charmer. You will—

BACHAN (*cutting her off*): Don't push it. Let them decide themselves.

(*The doorbell rings.*)

BACHAN: It must be the caterers. (*He exits.*)

(*Nirmal is tiding up the place. She unplugs the vacuum cleaner cord.*)

NIRMAL: Roop, would you please vacuum the stairs and the basement, and tidy up your room? Change your clothes. No jeans, please.

ROOP: No jeans?

NIRMAL: Nope! No jeans. Get ready.

(*The phone rings. Roop picks up the phone. He hands it over to Nirmal.*)

ROOP: It is for you.

(*Roop reluctantly picks up the vacuum cleaner and leaves. Nirmal is on the phone, and continues to tidy up the place. The lights go out, and slowly, they come back.*)

# SCENE TWO

*Saturday afternoon.*

*The Captain, Neelum, Bachan, Roop, and Neetu are sitting in the family room. Nirmal enters with a tray of desserts and tea and places it on the coffee table. She pours tea for everyone, and Neelum passes the cups around. From time to time, the desert plate is passed around.*

---

THE CAPTAIN: Nirmal ji$^2$, every dish was very delicious.

NEETU: Yes, Auntie ji, it was a very tasty lunch.

NEELUM: There was no need to go to this extent. We are family.

NIRMAL: You don't come here every day.

NEELUM: Your mother used to make the best *pakoras$^3$*.

NIRMAL: Those days seem like another life.

NEELUM: On the West Coast, it doesn't feel like you are in a foreign country.

---

2 *ji*. The term suggests a show of respect.
3 *pakoras*. A fried snack made out of chickpea flour, vegetables and spices.

NIRMAL: Here too. There are some areas but nothing like the West Coast.

BACHAN: Nirmal, remember when we came here? We had to drive forty or fifty miles to buy Indian groceries. Now you can get them at every corner in some neighborhoods.

THE CAPTAIN: Even the main stores carry many spices and other items.

BACHAN: Captain *Sahib*[4], are you still working somewhere? I understand you have retired from the military.

THE CAPTAIN: After retirement, I did join an IT company for five or six months.

NEELUM: After the military, it is difficult to work in the private sector. He was grumbling every day. Then, I said, "Just leave it."

THE CAPTAIN: The job was not the problem. It was the traveling time every day. Missus (*looking at Neelum*) refused to move there.

NEELUM (*softly*): My mother is not doing well.

NIRMAL (*with concern*): What happened?

---

4 **sahib**. The term suggests a show of respect.

NEELUM: Old age.

NIRMAL: Nothing serious?

NEELUM: No. Just weak eyesight, joint pain…

THE CAPTAIN: Neelum and Neetu are interested in opening a business here.

NEELUM: There is nothing like your own business.

NIRMAL: You can set your own hours.

NEELUM: What do you think, Roop?

ROOP (*caught off guard*): About what?

NEELUM: About opening your own business.

ROOP: It could be a good idea.

NEETU (*excitedly*): Mom, I think it is a wonderful idea. Otherwise, I have to go to college. They wouldn't honor my MBA here. Would they? (*She is looking at Roop for the answer.*)

ROOP: They might.

NEETU: How would I find out?

ROOP: You have to send in your certificates for evaluation.

BACHAN: When we came, they were considering our BA equal to high school, and an MA was considered equivalent to a BA. The evaluation rules might have changed now.

ROOP: Most of the foreign students have to repeat their master's degree here.

NEELUM: That's why Neetu says she wants to open a boutique.

THE CAPTAIN: Roop, how long does it take to complete a master's degree?

ROOP: It depends, between one and a half to two years.

NIRMAL: Even with the master's degree, there is no surety of jobs these days.

NEELUM: That's why Neetu is interested in opening her own business.

NIRMAL (*suddenly*): Roop, why don't you show Neetu around the house? She must be getting bored. Or go and put a movie on. We will come down there, too.

(*Roop gets up and waits for Neetu. Neetu looks at Neelum inquisitively. Neelum nods approvingly. Roop and Neetu exit.*)

THE CAPTAIN (*addressing Bachan*): You have a beautiful house. The location is nice. Not too far away from the city center yet a very quiet area.

NEELUM (*nodding in agreement*): A very nice location.

NIRMAL: This is our first house. We have been here for almost thirty years.

BACHAN: Usually, after a while, the residential areas become crowded with commercial properties. The layout of the streets is such that, so far, it has been saved.

NEELUM: Back home, we built a house on the outskirts of the city.

THE CAPTAIN: The cities are getting too crowded.

NEELUM: But the one in Neetu's name is in the middle of the city.

THE CAPTAIN: It generates a good monthly income.

NEELUM: She has been saving her money over the years. That is why she is interested in opening a boutique.

NIRMAL: That is a wonderful idea. She will do fine in business. She has a very outgoing personality.

BACHAN: Roop did look into some IT business, but now he is looking for a job.

NIRMAL: He has job offers already.

NEELUM: Work does take one far from home.

NIRMAL: Not all the time.

BACHAN: Roop can settle down wherever he decides or wherever he gets a job.

NIRMAL (*looking at The Captain*): It is up to the children. They have to decide.

BACHAN (*softly*): We do not want to force them one way or the other.

THE CAPTAIN (*adding hastily*): That is the best way. That is what I have been telling Neelum. Let the children decide. We should not force or influence them one way or other.

BACHAN: That is the best way.

NEELUM: Neetu is already worried that you can't get any help here. She didn't lift a finger back home. You know how things are there.

NIRMAL: She will get used to it. Everybody does.

NEELUM: She is learning how to cook. The other day, she made *aloo-gobbi*[5]. It was very tasty. I was telling her that these days you can get everything readymade here too.

(*Roop and Neetu enter.*)

NIRMAL (*to Roop*): You are back so soon! Why? (*To Neetu*) You didn't want to watch a movie?

NEETU (*lightly*): Auntie, they are old movies. I have seen all of them.

NIRMAL: Roop, both of you can go and get a new release from the store. Go. Go, Roop.

NEETU (*insisting*): No, Auntie. Thank you. We bought a few yesterday, didn't we, Mom?

NEELUM: We did, but we have not seen them yet.

NIRMAL (*firmly*): Go, Roop, you also get new movies. Go.

---

5  *aloo-gobbi*. Spicy dish made out of potatoes and cauliflower.

NEELUM: That is all right, Nirmal. We will sit here and talk. We haven't seen each other in a long time. Movies are always there.

NIRMAL (*enthusiastically*): Roop, Neetu wants to open a boutique. Don't you think it is a wonderful idea?

ROOP: Boutique?

NIRMAL: What do you think?

ROOP: If that is what Neetu is interested in.

NEETU: I am very excited about it. I can picture just how I want to organize it.

NEELUM: We have already contacted a tailor back home. Neetu wants to bring the latest fashions here.

NEETU (*excitedly*): Yes, Mom, the latest. (*To Nirmal*) Auntie, I want to bring all the new fashions here as soon as they come out.

NIRMAL: Such a wonderful idea! What do you think, Roop?

ROOP (*with surprise*): Me?

BACHAN: Fashion changes every day. The business can be very successful.

THE CAPTAIN: Owning a business, one has peace of mind. Whatever effort you put in, the reward is all yours.

NEELUM (*hastily*): In jobs, you are always at the mercy of others.

BACHAN: So too in business ownership.

NIRMAL (*looking at Bachan*): The job market goes through too many ups and downs.

BACHAN: Roop has a few job offers already.

NIRMAL (*looking at the Captain*): Children have to decide what they want for themselves.

(*The Captain is looking at his watch.*)

THE CAPTAIN: Bachan Sahib, now, give us permission to leave. (*He stands up from his seat.*) Nirmal ji, thank you for the delicious lunch. With God's grace, we will meet again. Roop, very nice to meet you, son.

NIRMAL (*surprised*): So soon?

NEELUM (*apologetically*): One of his friends has invited us; otherwise, we would have stayed longer. But we will meet again.

(*They bid goodbyes. Neetu, Neelum, and the Captain exit.*)

NIRMAL (*to herself*): I do not have any objections to opening a boutique. One can set one's own hours. Whatever hours and hard work you put in, you are rewarded for it.

ROOP: As long as I do not have to sit there.

NIRMAL (*exasperated*): You do not have to sit there. She seems like a very capable young lady.

ROOP: There are no servants here to open the boxes.

NIRMAL: The help can be arranged. (*To Bachan*) What do you think?

BACHAN: The girl is beautiful and from a good family. What is there not to like?

NIRMAL (*to Roop*): And you?

ROOP (*uneasily*): To me, it seems like she is not very interested. She could have watched an old movie with me. We could have spent more time together.

NIRMAL: Do not be silly. There will be plenty of time you can spend together. They are here for a few days. You can take her to the movies.

ROOP: And about the boutique; I do not see myself doing that type of work.

NIRMAL: She is the one who will be running it. You should appreciate that she wants to do something rather than moping around the house. Beside the boutique, you do like the girl. Don't you?

ROOP: What is there not to like? She is beautiful. (*Beseechingly*) But Mom, I do not know her.

NIRMAL: You will come to know her in due time.

ROOP: Look at the competition. There is a boutique at every corner. Besides, running a boutique is not easy work. You have to constantly deal with all sorts of people, imports, exports, sales, and everything else. Seven days a week, twenty-four hours a day, that is all one thinks; selling and buying, buying and selling, packing and unpacking, unpacking and packing…sooner or later, I will be dragged into it.

NIRMAL (*sharply*): Why you? Her mom and dad are here. In fact, her mom may be helping her all the time.

ROOP: Then, I will be running errands for all of them.

NIRMAL (*insisting*): Just think about it. Just think how much money there is in that business.

BACHAN (*abruptly*): Money! How much money do you need in life? You were never in need of anything. I did very well by you and Roop.

NIRMAL (*abashed*): Did I ever complain?

BACHAN: I never gave you any reason to complain, did I?

ROOP: I remember when I was in elementary school; Mom, your restaurant venture…

BACHAN (*brightly*): Yes, yes, I did not want to bring it up, but (*to Roop*) you did, and you have a point. (*To Nirmal*) Remember when you wanted to open the restaurant? You called it a takeout place. Who was buying and carrying those supplies day in and day out?

NIRMAL: I did not have any help.

ROOP (*emphatically*): That is the point, Mom. You think she is going to run the boutique by herself? We will all be dragged into it.

NIRMAL (*sharply*): You, neither of you, know how far people are going. You have no idea. Job! Job! These days, what is in a job?

ROOP: Mom, if you are so convinced that owning a business is the right thing, now that both of you are retired, you can try! But count me out.

BACHAN: Me too!

ROOP: And did they ask me what I want to do? How I feel about it?

NIRMAL: I told them that you have job offers.

ROOP: Running a boutique is not my kind of life. There is nothing wrong with it, Mom. It is hard work, but it is not for me.

NIRMAL (*with irritation*): Stop it, now! I get the picture. Forget about the boutique. What about the girl?

ROOP: What about her?

NIRMAL: Do you like her?

ROOP (*desperately*): Mother, how many times are you going to ask me? She is a beautiful girl, but I hardly know her.

NIRMAL: Then, get to know her. I did not know your father when we got married.

BACHAN: That is not true. Your *massi ji*[6] used to live in our village.

NIRMAL: My *massi ji* lived in your village. I didn't.

---

6 *massi ji*. Aunt.

BACHAN: She knew me, and your mother knew me.

NIRMAL: Did we ever meet?

BACHAN (*chuckling*): I knew where you went to college, what classes you attended, and when you skipped classes to see matinee movies with your friends.

NIRMAL (*surprised*): You knew all that!

BACHAN: We knew all that about all the girls. We used to hang out outside your college.

NIRMAL: My college!

BACHAN: All the time, but I did not know I would end up marrying you.

NIRMAL (*resignedly*): That is all you did, waste time.

BACHAN (*gaily*): I would not call it wasted time. It was a good investment. I knew everything about you before we got married.

NIRMAL: You call it an investment? Skipping classes and stalking girls!

BACHAN: That is all we did. Those were good times, before the age of cell phones and e-mail.

ROOP (*shock*ed): So, you would skip classes to hang around in front of the girls' college?

NIRMAL (*dismissingly*): Do not give him any ideas.

ROOP: It's too late, Mom. I'm almost done with my studies.

NIRMAL (*impatiently*): He is just telling tall tales, son. Do not listen to him.

BACHAN (*smiling*): No, I am not. It is all true.

ROOP: And here you want full details of my each second.

BACHAN: It is your mother, not I. Do not look at me!

NIRMAL: Oh, just—

BACHAN: Our mothers trusted us.

NIRMAL (*impatiently*): No, they trusted other people's daughters more than they trusted you. These days, the girls are throwing themselves all over the boys.

ROOP: That's not true. I don't see any girl throwing herself at me.

NIRMAL: Your time will come.

BACHAN (*brightly*): You have stayed under your mother's shadow for too long.

ROOP: I strongly believe that someday someone will walk into my life, or I will walk into her life.

NIRMAL (*hurt*): Yes, hold on to these dreams. You have to make things happen, the way I am trying to do for you, find a nice girl for you.

ROOP: Sometimes, you should let things happen in life rather than—

NIRMAL: Rather than what? Since when has it become a crime to try to bring a beautiful and educated girl into the family?

BACHAN (*seriously*): Nirmal, they have just met for the first time. Let us see how things unfold.

ROOP: Yes, Mom.

NIRMAL (*agitated*): You two! You will never let me live in peace.

BACHAN (*affectionately*): It is for your peace of mind, Nirmal. I am saying not to rush into any decision. That is all I am thinking of, your peace of mind.

(*Nirmal turns on the TV. Roop affectionately tries to put his arm around Nirmal. She pushes him away.*)

ROOP (*earnestly*): Mom, please!

(*Nirmal ignores them. She begins to collect the dishes.*)

*Curtain.*

# SCENE THREE

*Friday afternoon.*

*Break room in the campus cafeteria. It has a few chairs and tables, a microwave, and a vending machine.*

*Preet is sitting in corner. Her bags and papers are scattered on the table. She is dressed simply and her hair is pulled back. Roop watches her for a few minutes from the other side of the cafeteria. He walks over to her table.*

---

ROOP: Do you mind if I join you?

PREET (*reluctantly*): You have walked all the way. You might as well sit down.

(*He pulls out the chair and sits down opposite her. She is not paying any attention to him and keeps going through the papers.*)

ROOP (*inquisitively*): I haven't seen you around the campus before.

PREET: I'm new here.

ROOP: Is this your first year here? Are you from the West Coast?

PREET: What coast?

ROOP: I mean, are you from Vancouver side?

PREET: No.

ROOP: So, you are a prairie girl.

PREET: What girl?

ROOP: From the mid provinces.

PREET: No.

ROOP: So, are you from this province?

PREET: No.

ROOP: So, why don't you tell me?

PREET (*irritated*): Tell you what?

ROOP: Since you are new here, where are you from?

PREET (*sharply*): Just ask me, and I will tell you. You are the one playing guessing games.

ROOP: So, tell me!

PREET: Tell you what?

ROOP: Where are you from?

PREET: A month or so ago, I got off the plane from India, and here I am.

ROOP (*surprised*): By yourself?

PREET (*sarcastically*): Why? Do you think I can't get off the plane by myself?

ROOP: I mean, did anyone accompany you?

PREET: Yes, someone was with me.

ROOP: Oh, I see.

PREET (*agitated with the papers*): You see what?

ROOP: That someone was with you.

PREET: Yes, it was all his idea, as if there were no good colleges and universities at home. I was doing just fine there, but once an idea gets in his head, there's no taking it back. He can be stubborn sometimes.

ROOP (*with concern*): That is no way to treat a girl, to impose on her. Your family didn't say anything?

PREET: He is my family.

ROOP: Sorry.

PREET: What do you mean?

ROOP: I am sorry that you have a family member who would impose his wishes on you.

PREET: He is no member of anything. He is the family. He thinks it is best for me to get an education from a prestigious, foreign university. He will go back and sit in the warm sun, leaving me behind in this shiver land. I hear it gets very cold here.

ROOP: It does get cold in the winters.

PREET: Last year, during the winter, he took me to Kashmir, so I could experience the snow, and to prepare me for the winter.

ROOP: That was very nice of him.

PREET (*irritated*): Nice of him? Nice of him!

ROOP (*baffled*): Yes, to prepare for—

PREET: Two weeks preparation for two years of this!

ROOP: Two years?

PREET: I joined the master's program here.

ROOP: Master's! What subject?

PREET: I'm getting my MBA.

ROOP: MBA?

PREET (*annoyed*): Can't you find your own words?

ROOP: My own words?

PREET (*exasperated*): Never mind.

ROOP: Here we are, two strangers! We are talking as if we have known each other for long time. Sometimes it is easy to talk to strangers. (*He pauses*) It seems as though we have met before.

PREET: Not a chance.

ROOP: No?

PREET: Believe me. I would have remembered you. I can count on my fingers all the foreigners I have met in my entire life.

ROOP: You don't seem to think much of foreigners, do you?

PREET: I did not say anything one way or the other.

ROOP: Since you have met one foreigner now, what do you think?

PREET: Think of what?

ROOP: Of foreigners?

PREET: You consider yourself a foreigner?

ROOP: I am a foreigner in your eyes. Aren't I?

PREET: So you are. But you seem to be all right.

ROOP: Are you staying at campus?

PREET: Yes, when classes start.

ROOP: Not now, but you will be staying on campus when classes start?

PREET: Why do you always repeat what I say?

ROOP: Do I?

PREET: Never mind. Where are you from?

ROOP: I grew up here, in this town.

PREET: So, you are a local!

ROOP: You could say that.

PREET: Did you ever visit back home?

ROOP: Once, actually twice. (*He pauses*) Would you like coffee or tea?

PREET: No, thank you. Didn't you just finish two cups of coffee?

ROOP (*surprised*): Were you watching me?

PREET: You don't see any crowds here, do you?

ROOP: It is amazing! I just can't shake the feeling that we have met somewhere before.

PREET (*firmly*): You can shake off that feeling. As I said before, I would have remembered. What is eating you up?

ROOP (*laughing uneasily*): Eating me up?

PREET: What is bothering you?

ROOP: How do you know something is bothering me?

PREET: For the past hour, you have been sitting in an empty cafeteria swooning over cups of coffee. Not a very productive or exciting way to spend time, is it?

ROOP: Nothing. It's nothing. (*He pauses. Then, hesitantly*) I don't want—

PREET: You don't have to talk if you don't want to.

ROOP: Maybe some other time. Let me know if you need help. Here is my cell number.

(*He writes down the number on a piece of paper and places it in front of her.*)

PREET: Well, he says, be cautious; people don't have to know that I am new here.

ROOP: That is a good advice.

PREET: Yes, he is full of good advice.

ROOP: Call me in case of an emergency.

PREET (*hesitantly taking the piece of paper*): Thank you.

ROOP: You don't have to give me yours if you don't want to.

PREET: Thank you. He won't like it since we have just met.

ROOP: He doesn't have to know it.

PREET: But he will.

ROOP: I won't tell him. As a matter of fact, I may never see him.

PREET: But I will.

ROOP (*gently*): Of course, you will see him. You are his family.

PREET: That's not what I mean. I mean I will end up telling him about this meeting.

ROOP: Why?

PREET (*shrugs*): That's the way it is. It will just come out. I met this boy…and so on.

ROOP: Why would you do that?

PREET (*vaguely*): That is the way it is.

ROOP: Just now, I got the impression that he—

PREET (*wearily*): Oh, I am just mad at him for—

ROOP: Bringing you here?

PREET: You can say that, among other things. My grand-mother used to say he is mule headed. Once things get in his head, there is no turning him back. He can be a force…he can…he is strong minded, hard headed.

ROOP (*uneasily*): So, will he be angry with you just because you talked to me?

PREET: Oh, no. No, he doesn't get mad often. He just wants me to use common sense.

ROOP: He seems like a strict person.

PREET: No, he is not.

ROOP: From your conversation, it seems that way.

PREET: He is not strict.

ROOP: No?

PREET: He thinks he is doing all this for my own good, out of love.

ROOP: Yes. To me, he seems like a dictator.

PREET: No, no! That he is not. He is no dictator.

ROOP: Sending you here against your wishes and giving you all these instructions, it looks like a dictatorship.

PREET: As I said, he gets all these ideas in his head.

ROOP: But, you have to suffer!

PREET: Suffer, no…he will suffer more.

ROOP: How so?

PREET: I will be busy with my studies. (*As if to herself*) He will be all alone there. I don't like that a bit. I don't like it. He can be mule headed as grandmother used to say. It is all for my own good. He says he can't keep me with him always. I have to go sooner or later. He can be stubborn sometimes.

ROOP: It is very nice of you to take it that way. Here, kids would walk out of the house.

PREET (*distressed*): I am out of the house already.

ROOP: Sorry. I didn't mean to hurt you.

PREET (*quietly*): Just for once, if he would let me live there with him.

(*Preet keeps checking her phone.*)

PREET (*as if waking up*): Why are you here? What do you do?

ROOP: I don't know. I will graduate at the end of this semester. Then—

PREET: That goes around here a lot, doesn't it?

ROOP: What do you mean?

PREET: "I don't know" seems to be the favorite phrase here. My aunt's two children, my cousins, you ask them what they want to study, "What you want to do?" And they say, "I don't know."

ROOP: That's funny.

PREET: I don't see anything funny in this. But, they do have a long list of things that they don't want to do.

ROOP: That will narrow the field. You seem very sure of yourself.

PREET (*offended*): No, I am not.

ROOP: Do you never say I don't know?

PREET: No!

ROOP (*gaily*): So, you know everything? Impossible!

PREET (*severely*): No, I don't know everything, but one can find out. If I can't find out myself, I will ask some-one, or I will say that I am not sure. To me, it seems simply rubbish to say, "I don't know."

ROOP: Rubbish! That's a very strong word to use.

PREET: I don't mean to offend you.

ROOP (*smiling*): From now on, I will say "I am not sure."

PREET: Not too much of "I am not sure." Then, they will think you don't know what you are doing.

ROOP: There's no winning. Is there?

PREET (*shakes her head*): Not really!

ROOP: I have two choices. I can start a job or stay in school.

PREET: Do your parents support you?

ROOP: On this account, they do.

PREET: Lucky you, you can choose.

ROOP: You seem very sure of your choice.

PREET: That needs to be seen. Back home I was, but if I end up staying here, I may change my mind.

ROOP: Here you are. You aren't sure yourself after all, are you?

PREET: I am sure for now, but if the circumstances change, I will do something else. What do I care? He is paying for it.

ROOP: Oh, that's nice of him.

PREET: Nice of him! Nice of him! This is the least he can do. He will go back in a few days and sit in the warm sun. I will be here in the shiver land.

ROOP: It is good to know I am not the only one.

PREET: Only one of what?

ROOP: Being railed into doing something I don't want to do.

PREET: For example?

ROOP (*uneasily*): My parents, especially my mom… never mind. (*He hesitates*) It's nothing like your situation getting shipped to a new country; it's nothing like that…

PREET (*gently*): You are upset, so it must be serious.

ROOP (*abruptly*): Well, it is my mom more than my father. She has this girl in her mind, her friend's daughter. Well…I…

PREET: You don't like her because you don't like her?
Or because she is your parents' choice?

ROOP: What do you mean?

PREET: Is she ugly?

ROOP: No. She is good looking, very beautiful.

PREET: Is she educated?

ROOP: Yes.

PREET: Is she from a good family?

ROOP: Yes.

PREET: Is she is from here?

ROOP: Well, her parents immigrated to Canada a year
or so ago.

PREET: Here?

ROOP: West Coast.

PREET: Vancouver?

ROOP: Yes.

PREET: Then, what is wrong with her? She seems to have all the credentials parents are looking for in girls for their sons.

ROOP: So, do you think I should say yes?

PREET (*taken aback*): I don't know you well, and I don't know the girl. I can't be the matchmaker. If it feels right in your heart, then you should say yes.

ROOP (*as if to himself*): That's it. Something is missing, but I don't know what. Mom keeps on asking me. I don't know myself. I wish they would back off.

PREET: They are not forcing you, are they?

ROOP: Look who is talking about being forced. Being shipped to a foreign country; that's being forced.

PREET (*fiercely*): Well, he will never force me to marry or try to convince me. He knows me better. He will do the right thing by me. He will never force me. He has no hidden motive but my happiness.

ROOP (*baffled*): Just now, you were calling him stubborn!

PREET: So he is, in many ways. But not when it comes to marriage. He will never force me.

ROOP: You are lucky.

PREET: I don't know about that.

ROOP: Does he have somebody in mind?

PREET (*complacently*): He talks about this boy, his friend's son he met long time ago when he was a young boy. But he wants to wait and see. He says people change.

ROOP: What about you?

PREET: What about me?

ROOP: So, you have somebody in mind?

PREET: Me? No! I believe in fate. At the right time, the right person will cross my way.

ROOP (*amazed*): And will you know when it happens?

PREET: I hope so. Someday.

ROOP: That's it. I don't have someday. They are ready to put a noose around my neck.

PREET (*astonished*): Noose, you say!

ROOP (*drily*): What else can I say? (*He pauses*) You're sure we have not met before?

PREET (*insisting*): I am pretty sure. I remember all the foreign people I have ever met. It is not so many that I would get confused.

ROOP: I feel like running away from home.

PREET: You don't want to do that. You will worry your parents.

ROOP: I don't know how to put some sense into them. I don't know what to say.

PREET: Say you want to think about it.

ROOP: Mom says, "What is there to think about it?"

PREET: I agree with her.

ROOP (*shocked*): You agree with her!

PREET: Either you like the girl, or you don't like the girl.

ROOP (*raising his voice*): Nobody seems to understand that my point is I hardly know the girl. Liking or not liking is the next step.

PREET: Why are you shouting at me?

ROOP (*nervously*): I am sorry.

PREET (*slowly*): It is your family matter. The only thing I can say is that you should get to know the girl. It is your personal matter. I do not want to interfere by suggesting anything.

ROOP: They want an answer. No time for that. I have not even finished my studies. I have not decided on a job.

PREET: Then, tell them so, and in the meantime, talk to the girl and get to know her.

ROOP (*relieved*): It may work.

PREET: What may work?

ROOP: That I want to wait until I finish my studies and decide on a job. Thank you.

PREET (*surprised*): That is all right. But what did I do? (*Preet checks her watch. Her phone rings. To Roop*) Excuse me. (*She speaks into the phone*) When? Hold for a minute? (*Addressing Roop*) What is the name of this building? The street? (*Roop writes the answers on the paper that is lying on the table.*) I will be out in a minute. (*She puts the phone away.*) He is outside waiting for me. (*She collects her things in rush.*)

Roop: Will I see you again?

Preet: Classes start in a week. Good luck with your mom.

(*Preet collects her belongings in a hurry and leaves. Roop gets up from his chair.*)

Roop: Your name? What is your name?

(*His voice lingers behind her. She does not hear him. As Preet is leaving, a paper falls on the floor. She exits. Roop picks up piece of paper from the floor.*)

Roop: My phone number! She dropped my phone number! She forgot my phone number! Oh no!

*Curtain.*

# SCENE FOUR

*Saturday. Late in the afternoon. Family room. Nirmal is on the phone. Roop enters. He sits beside Nirmal and scans through reading materials. She is engrossed in the conversation. He goes to the computer desk, gets up and walks around restlessly. As soon as Nirmal ends the conversation:*

---

ROOP: Mom, where is Dad?

NIRMAL: He went to pick up Chacha ji[7].

ROOP: Chacha ji?

NIRMAL: Do you remember him? The one from our village.

ROOP: Yes, I do remember. He used to take me around all over the village and fields.

NIRMAL: Yes, the same. Apparently, he came along with his daughter. She will be joining the university here.

ROOP: University? Here?

NIRMAL: That's what your father told me.

---

7  **chachaji**. Father's younger brother in particular, or younger male cousin or father's friend.

ROOP: Are they staying with us?

NIRMAL: They are staying with his sister-in-law. Your lunch is on the dining table.

ROOP: I had lunch in the cafeteria. When are they coming?

NIRMAL: Anytime. (*Getting up and putting the reading material aside. Voices and laughter are heard in the background.*) I think they are here.

(*Chacha ji and Bachan enter. Chacha ji joins his palms and bows his head, and Nirmal responds the same way. He shakes hands with Roop.*)

CHACHA JI (*radiantly*): You look the same, Nirmal. (*Nirmal nods her head shyly*) You have not changed a bit. And here, my boy, Roop, (*patting Roop's shoulder*) you have grown up since the last time I saw you.

(*As they are seating themselves, Nirmal exits.*)

CHACHA JI: So, my boy, your dad told me that that you are studying to be a nuclear engineer.

ROOP (*uneasily*): Yes, Chacha ji.

CHACHA JI: I've never heard about nuclear engineering.

BACHAN: During our day, every other person was studying to be either a civil, mechanical, or electrical engineer.

CHACHA JI (*firmly*): That is so true.

ROOP: Chacha ji, these days, we have many more choices.

CHACHA JI: So it seems, son. For new times, new fields of study.

(*Nirmal enters with tea and snacks.*)

BACHAN: Tea! (*Looking at Chacha ji*) What about a drink?

CHACHA JI: Maybe later. It is not every day that I get a chance to drink tea made by Nirmal.

NIRMAL (*smiling*): *Veer ji*[8], you are as charming as ever.

CHACHA JI (*looking around*): Nirmal, it is a beautiful home. These days, you cannot find most of these artifacts in the markets.

BACHAN: Only miniatures, and those too only in museums or art shows.

---

8 *veer ji.* Brother.

(*Nirmal serves tea to everyone, and from time to time, the snacks are passed around.*)

BACHAN: There used to be rows and rows of clay pots, all sizes and shapes. You cannot find them anywhere.

NIRMAL: And the fridge water; fridge water is no match for the water from the clay pot. The taste is so unique.

CHACHA JI: Especially when it is covered with the jute bag. (*Looking around with enthusiasm*) Nirmal, you have brought a glimpse of Punjab to this home.

BACHAN: She has an uncanny sense of where each piece belongs. When she brings something home, it fits like a glove.

NIRMAL: Most of the time, I buy in spite of your griping.

BACHAN: I think we already have more than we need.

NIRMAL (*firmly*): These things are not for needs.

BACHAN: Then what are they for?

CHACHA JI (*thoughtfully*): They are to please the eye and the soul.

NIRMAL (*unruffled*): Tell him, *Veer ji.*

BACHAN: Things do not please the soul.

NIRMAL: If it was up to you, we would only have the bare necessities. Bare walls!

BACHAN (*reflectively*): I do not understand all this. It is our home; people make it a home. It is how they treat each other that makes it home. It is not a little museum.

NIRMAL (*irritated*): You can be impossible!

BACHAN: That is why I never say anything about these things.

NIRMAL (*dryly*): And let us keep it that way.

BACHAN (*in a conciliatory tone*): Do not get angry with me. I am just saying that I do not understand all this.

CHACHA JI (*looking around*): It does look very nice. Nirmal, it feels like home; a home away from home. It feels like old times, all of us sitting here together.

ROOP (*supportively*): Mom, you have done a wonderful job decorating.

CHACHA JI: Women are the ones who run the home. We have to let them have their way.

NIRMAL (*firmly*): Tell him, *Veer ji*. He thinks it is an easy job.

BACHAN: I have never said it is an easy job.

ROOP: Mom, you do a wonderful job.

CHACHA JI (*sorrowfully*): God bless her soul, my dear wife. When she was alive, she ran the house like a well-oiled machine. (*Rebounding with a soft smile*) But my mother also stepped aside. She used to say, "I had my time. Now, it is time for new generation." My wife never made her feel neglected. My mother used to say no daughter could have been more loving. I was a lucky man. She was a gentle soul, my wife.

NIRMAL (*sympathetically*): What happened? I knew she was sick for some time.

CHACHA JI (*staring on the floor*): Breast cancer.

NIRMAL: Oh!

CHACHA JI: God's will.

NIRMAL: And, raising a daughter without your wife—

BACHAN (*to Chacha ji*): *Bai*[9], it must be difficult for you to raise a child without a mother.

CHACHA JI: My mother was a tremendous help.

NIRMAL: Of course.

CHACHA JI: Yes, good women run the house, make the old souls slide out of this life with dignity and love. In old times, that is what people focused on…the family background, the honor—

NIRMAL: *Veer ji*, those things matter now, too.

CHACHA JI: Of course they do, but times have changed.

BACHAN: So true.

CHACHA JI: In the old times, nobody used to know the names of the daughter-in-laws in the communities. They were known by the name of their towns or villages.

BACHAN: That is so true.

---

9 **bai**. Friend, brother.

CHACHA JI: All the ones from mother's generation…
come to think of it, I did not know their names…but I
knew where they were from…yes, that was the way it
was…their behavior was considered a direct reflection
on their families. Yes, that was the way it was, was it
not Bachan?

BACHAN: Yes, you are right. I didn't know my mother's name for a long time. Everyone used to call her
*Chack Wali.*

ROOP: What does that mean?

BACHAN: My mother was from the village named
*Chack,* and *wali* means from or belong to; thus,
*Chackan Wali* means one from the village *Chack.*

ROOP: What if there were two from the same village?

BACHAN: Then, they differentiate by saying *Choti*,
meaning younger, and *Badhi*, meaning older.

CHACHA JI (*wearily*): Everything is misplaced. Not only
misplaced, it is shifting like mercury; you can't put
your finger on it. Today, you see people poking each
other's ribs with their elbows in temple's *langar[10]*, but
at home, they count every morsel of food on old parents' plates…

---

10 *langar*. Kitchen.

BACHAN: I have seen this with my own eyes.

NIRMAL (*protesting*): You have seen no such thing.

BACHAN (*with emphasis*): I have seen with my own two eyes. Yes, I have.

NIRMAL: What have you seen?

BACHAN: You know the family who used to live in the house at the end of our street?

NIRMAL: What about them?

BACHAN: Many times, I saw old parents dragging the grocery cart in the snow. Sometimes, I used to give them a ride. Now, the fridge is always full.

NIRMAL (*dryly*): Since when did you start checking on another family's fridge?

BACHAN: You do not have to check. It is right there in the family room. Every time someone opens it, one can see what is there.

NIRMAL (*adding hastily*): Maybe that was a way to make them spend some of their money. I heard he was wasting it anyways.

BACHAN: Wasting?

NIRMAL: I heard he used to drink.

BACHAN: Who does not? But I never saw him drunk.

NIRMAL: Nobody in his right mind would get drunk and walk in the streets.

BACHAN: It may be true. And if it were, then they should have asked them for a monetary contribution up front. Do not make old people push grocery carts in the snow. How much does it cost to give *dal–roti*[11] to two people? Or better yet, arrange a separate accommodation.

NIRMAL: Everyone deserves one's own place, big or small.

BACHAN: I agree. That is why we have decided to live by ourselves.

ROOP: What if you get sick?

NIRMAL: When that time comes, we will see.

ROOP: You won't stay with me?

NIRMAL: No.

ROOP (*surprised*): No?

---

11 *dal-roti*. *Dal* is a spicy lentil/bean soup. *Roti* is flat bread. The term *dal-roti* is used to mean food in general.

BACHAN: We have decided that already.

(*There is silence.*)

CHACHA JI (*to Nirmal*): What happened to the parents?

NIRMAL (*caught off guard*): Who?

CHACHA JI: The family down the road.

BACHAN: Two years ago, their mother died, and then the father returned home for a visit. There, he passed away. I think he had heart attack.

NIRMAL (*whispering*): You do not know the other family's situation.

BACHAN (*emphatically*): I have said what I saw. And, *Bai,* you are right. These days, boys do not have any backbone. One day, we were visiting them and the mother said something...the son jumped up like a lion...his wife was sitting there, rolling her big eyes... I don't know what she whispered...blinked her eyes or sneezed...like Pavlov's dog, he was all over his mother...for no reason.

NIRMAL (*to Bachan*): With all of your education, at least, you remember Pavlov's dog. All those years in the college were not wasted after all.

CHACHA JI: It must be building up for some time.

BACHAN: Our generation…we would have never dared to raise our voice in front of our parents.

CHACHA JI: That is true. I remember if I ever did, my wife would step in and take their side, and that is a sign of a good woman. When the man gets out of the line, it's a woman that brings him back on the right path.

ROOP: Things are not that bad. I will not let anyone mistreat my parents.

CHACHA JI (*gaily*): You won't know what hit you, my son. You won't know a thing.

BACHAN: All sons before you have sworn to the same.

NIRMAL (*decisively*): I did not give you any reason.

BACHAN: Never! And my mother adored you, didn't she?

NIRMAL: I was lucky that way.

BACHAN (*baffled*): You were lucky that way! (*Protesting*) And in what way are you unlucky?

NIRMAL (*dryly*): Don't be so sensitive—

ROOP: I would know if someone disrespected my parents.

CHACHA JI (*smiling*): You won't know a thing, my boy. You won't know what hit you. You won't know a thing. (*Animating with his hands*) When the peacock dance is done in front of you, when the tear rivers are emptied on your pillow, you won't know a thing.

ROOP (*protesting*): As I understand, your spouses didn't give you any reason. Why then? You—

CHACHA JI (*tenderly making a point*): Why? Why? Son, you ask me why? First, we have seen and heard stories about the women squabbling with each other. Mother used to say, in old times, women would fight among themselves, but by the time the men came home they acted as if nothing had happened.

NIRMAL: They tried to get along because they knew that they had to live together. They did not have any choice.

CHACHA JI (*as if to himself*): Mother used to say the house is not destroyed by the hands of a man. It is a woman who destroys the house. A good woman will save the house at any cost.

BACHAN: If there is anything to be saved, that is!

CHACHA JI: That is true. Sometimes it is beyond women… some men are no good. Only God can save them.

BACHAN (*looking at Chacha ji*): And we know a few men like that, don't we?

CHACHA JI: Sure, we do. We don't have to go far. In our own village, there are one or two men who have destroyed everything that took generations to build.

BACHAN: What can a poor woman do in that case, when one is bent on destroying everything?

NIRMAL: Then, women are stuck with raising the children.

BACHAN: These days, at least, they can find some sort of job. In the past, they would end up back at their parents' house.

CHACHA JI: Sometimes it was worse compared to the situation in their own houses.

NIRMAL: The sisters-in-law reminded them every day in whose house they were living.

BACHAN: And poor girls worked like servants until they died.

ROOP: Times have changed. The girls get equal education.

CHACHA JI (*enthusiastically*): Equal? Equal! You say equal, my son? Girls are surpassing boys in education!

NIRMAL: That is true.

CHACHA JI: No doubt. Not only that, but these days the boys are also weak.

ROOP (*with surprise*): Weak?

CHACHA JI (*to Roop, as if telling a story*): In old times, there was fear; fear of society, of community, and above all of God; and men were strong willed. They gave honor to their mothers and sisters, and cared for and protected their wives and children. They were strong. They maintained the balancing act most of the time. Today, the boys are feeble minded.

ROOP (*protesting*): You underestimate us, Chacha ji.

CHACHA JI (*gently*): Son, I did not say there is a lack of intelligence or wisdom.

ROOP: Then what?

CHACHA JI: A lack of common sense.

ROOP (*perplexed*): A lack of common sense!

CHACHA JI: And no backbone.

ROOP (*baffled*): No backbone!

CHACHA JI: Either the parents are thrown out or the wife and children are thrown out. I am telling you, nothing but spineless creatures.

ROOP: Spineless creatures! (*Appalled*) How can you say that, Chacha ji?

CHACHA JI: I have seen too much pain on both sides. One more thing, (*to Bachan*) our generation…during our time, no son would dare to disrespect his parents. Agree or disagree, follow their advice or not, but disrespect, (*nodding his head*) that was out of the question.

BACHAN: Times have changed.

CHACHA JI: I was blessed with two good and honest women. Mother used to say, Son, lying, manipulation, and cheating are like rust. Sooner or later, they will wear a relationship down. Two good women, God bless their souls.

BACHAN: Times have changed.

CHACHA JI (*reflectively*): Mother used to say the new generation's women are quiet, but they pour venom into men's hearts...slowly, slowly it spreads around. At that time, I could not figure out what she was trying to say. Now, I see what is going around...men talking to their wives, sisters, and mothers like mad dogs have bitten them...the language I hear...an honorable man would never say those things to any woman, let alone to the women in his own family.

NIRMAL (*tensely*): These days, it is difficult to settle down in a new house. Expectations are very high. One is expected to make a living, and then come home and do all the housework and be everything to everybody around.

ROOP: Sometimes parents can be so cruel as well. I met a girl on campus. It seems she was brought here against her wishes.

NIRMAL: Did she say that to you?

ROOP: No, not in so many words.

NIRMAL: Did she tell you why she was compelled to come here?

ROOP: For studies.

CHACHA JI (*as if to himself*): I wonder if my *beti*[12] feels that way about me. It is unbearable for me to leave her so far away. I hope I am doing the right thing.

(*The phone rings and Roop picks it up. After listening to who is on the other end, he hands the phone to Nirmal. She exits with the phone.*)

BACHAN: *Bai*, you should not worry about *beti*. We are here. We are her family, too. It is getting dark. Let us all have a drink.

(*Bachan prepares the drinks. Slowly the lights dim and the curtain is drawn.*)

*Interval.*

---

12 ***beti.*** Daughter

# SCENE FIVE

*The family room. Saturday, late evening. The atmosphere is relaxed. There are drinks on the table. Bachan and Chacha ji are drinking. Roop is sitting at the computer table. Chacha ji is more at ease than the others. Nirmal enters.)*

---

CHACHA JI: Roop, son. Here. (*He offers Roop a drink.*) You must give your Chacha ji company.

NIRMAL (*hastily*): *Veer ji*, Roop rarely drinks.

ROOP: Excuse me, Chacha ji. Maybe some other time. I need to catch up with my studies.

CHACHA JI: Now, we don't want to interfere with your studies, do we? Are you leaving your Chacha ji?

ROOP: No, not right now. Later I have to do some reading for my history class.

CHACHA JI: History class? One just needs to read the history of one kingdom and follow its tentacles all over the earth.

ROOP (*surprised*): Just one kingdom?

CHACHA JI (*firmly*): Just one.

ROOP: One!

CHACHA JI (*emphatically*). And that kingdom, my son, is Great Britain.

ROOP: Britain?

CHACHA JI: The one and only Great Britain.

ROOP: I am taking a Native Indian history class.

NIRMAL: Why do you need history class?

ROOP: To fulfill the liberal arts requirements.

CHACHA JI: Native Indians, American Indians, West Indians, East Indians…regardless what corner of the globe, or what people…all roads end up there or go through them.

ROOP: Chacha ji, that is a bit of an exaggeration.

NIRMAL (*bitterly*): The *firangi*[13] mind is the most corrupt mind, or I should say foxy mind, cunning mind. It is. There is no doubt about it in my mind.

ROOP: Mom, don't you think it is a bit extreme?

---

13 ***firangi***. Slang for white foreigner used in India when it was under British rule.

(*Phone rings. Nirmal answers it. She exits while on the phone.*)

BACHAN: Son, don't be harsh on your mother. She lost her younger brother at LOC[14.]

ROOP: That was thoughtless of me.

CHACHA JI: What a promising young man he was! (*To Roop*) Son, your mother is right. First, wherever they set their feet, they brought unimaginable destruction. They destroyed the local industries and shipped resources to the motherland. Then, when they left, they left behind divisions that pit neighbor against neighbor, and those divisions will last until the end of this world.

ROOP: You must agree that they introduced democracy in the world.

BACHAN: Roop, *Bai* is right on this point. Just look at the map of the world. Wherever there is bloodshed, directly or indirectly, their hand is behind it. Just look at the carnage...there is no end. It will be the same for centuries to come. It is the divisions, the sores that they have left behind that will fester until the last day.

---

14 **LOC**. The term Line of Control (LOC) refers to the military control line between the Indian and Pakistani controlled parts of the state of Jammu and Kashmir.

Roop: There may be some truth to this, but they left the infrastructure…the roads, the railways, the educational and court systems…the industries—

Chacha Ji: Did those societies exist in a void? They had their systems…their homegrown systems that served those societies very well.

Bachan: *Bai* is right. Societies do not exist in a void.

(*Nirmal returns with a bowl of vegetables. She covers her lap with a towel and prepares them for cooking.*)

Chacha Ji: Nations are like people, my son. Leave them alone, and they will find their own way. They develop resiliency; they grow and develop their own systems. Just like people; if you keep on tampering with them, they develop brittleness rather than resiliency and strength.

Bachan: The children here read things like *White Man's Burden.* They think the rest of the world used to live in jungles.

Nirmal (*indignantly*): If you ask me, it is not white man's burden. Rather, it is the burden of the white man that people have been carrying all over the globe.

Roop: Mom, there are some historical facts.

CHACHA JI: History? History is made by people who write history, and history is made by those who teach that history.

BACHAN: It is also made by those who pass it on without questioning it.

ROOP: European thinkers are the ones who came up with ideas of democracy and personal freedom.

BACHAN: Many indigenous societies had systems of justice, education, and government themselves.

ROOP (*sardonically*): Systems like cutting hands for stealing!

NIRMAL (*indifferently*): I do not see what all this fuss is about. A common man gets up in the morning and goes to work, so he can provide for his family, pay his bills, and take care of his responsibilities. It makes no difference to an ordinary person what type of government the country has—democracy, dictatorship, socialist, communist—in the end, they are all the same for an ordinary person as long as one has the means to provide for one's family.

ROOP: Oh, Mom. How can you say this?

CHACHA JI: Nirmal, you are right about the fate of the common man. But, if the common man gets caught up between these systems, may God help the common man.

BACHAN: We have come from one free country to another and have escaped the turmoil that is going on in other parts of the world.

CHACHA JI: This is true. Some places, the families are uprooted again and again, generation after generation. The fate of the common man has nothing common about it.

ROOP: Mom, the women in other countries don't have all the freedoms.

NIRMAL: Women are not completely free in any country, in any society, anywhere on this earth.

ROOP: You have freedom here. In the way you dress, to vote, to get an education…

NIRMAL: Only within the boundaries of certain morals.

ROOP (*perplexed*): No one is asking you to wear a *burka*[15], Mom. You are free to do whatever you want to do.

---

15 **burka.** A head to toe dress Muslim women wear to cover themselves.

NIRMAL (*firmly, with even tone*): As I said, only within the boundaries of certain morals, and all societies have set of morals for women. The difference is the degree. All societies attach the yardstick of morality to the behavior of their women regardless of where they are…east, west, north, or south. It is the same all over the world.

ROOP (*hastily*): Not in the twenty-first century, Mom!

NIRMAL: Women carry the burden of morality on their shoulders; or rather, they are burdened with morality.

ROOP: You can vote and let your voice be heard.

NIRMAL: My voice? Vote? What would my vote do? Would it change anything?

ROOP: Your vote matters, Mom. Every vote matters.

BACHAN: Ask your mother; when was the last time she voted?

NIRMAL: Never.

ROOP (*surprised*): Mom, never?

NIRMAL: They are all the same.

ROOP (*exasperated*): Oh, Mom. They are not all the same. How can you say that?

NIRMAL: Because that is the truth. They sing a different tune to get into the office. Once they get there, they are all the same.

ROOP: Oh, Mom. How can you think that way?

CHACHA JI: I do not know how things are here, but back home, it is true. All of them are corrupt. Whosoever comes in becomes busy lining one's own pockets, regardless of the party. There is no choice. They are all the same…no choice at all, only the illusion of change.

BACHAN (*to Nirmal*): Now, that is one of the places where your common man has no choice.

NIRMAL: That is why I tell you…vote? Vote for what? They are all the same.

ROOP: Not here, Mom. Here things are different. Each party has its own platform. Who is in office does matter. Here things get done.

BACHAN: When something gets stuck in your mother's mind, it is difficult to change.

CHACHA JI: She is right.

BACHAN (*to Chacha ji*): Not you too!

CHACHA JI: As I said, I do not know how things are here, but she is right. This is what happens back home. Every election!

ROOP (*firmly*): Then, people should vote them out of office. They have the choice.

CHACHA JI: It is not that easy. Vote them out to bring in whom? They are all the same.

ROOP: Not you too, Chacha ji.

NIRMAL: They are all the same. They will do and say anything to get your vote. They are not going to make a fool of me.

BACHAN (*smiling*): So you have been saving your votes to do what? There is no cumulative impact of your restraint. It is not like hoarding money.

NIRMAL: Everything is a joke to you.

BACHAN: On the contrary, I am being very serious. How many people on this earth wish that they could have the right to vote?

NIRMAL: My one vote will not make a difference.

ROOP: But, Mom, it does. It does make a difference.

(*The phone rings. Roop picks it up and exits with the phone. There is pause.*)

CHACHA JI: I thought you were a woman of shrewd judgement. I am disappointed in you. Nirmal, I am very disappointed.

NIRMAL (*baffled*): How so, *Veer ji*?

CHACHA JI: I thought you could see through a person.

NIRMAL: *Veer ji*, I have no idea what you are talking about.

CHACHA JI (*with renewed alertness*): Let me tell you, Nirmal. Let me be frank, very frank. If you promise me, you won't mind if I cross the line.

BACHAN (*chuckling*): It depends on what line you are thinking to cross.

CHACHA JI: What a thing to say! How can you say that once she got married to you? Though in my heart, I always wondered why. But I have honored her wishes. Haven't I, Nirmal?

NIRMAL (*nodding her head*): Yes. Yes you have.

CHACHA JI: Have I ever crossed the line, even in words?

NIRMAL (*lightly*): Now, now, let us stay focused on the issue at hand. (*She looks at her husband*) He does not mean anything by all this.

CHACHA JI (*sipping his drink*): Where were we?

BACHAN (*looking at Nirmal and smiling*): You were talking about Nirmal's judgement.

CHACHA JI: Oh, yes, yes, (*turning toward Nirmal*) your judgment. You are an intelligent woman, an intelligent and educated woman. You are also a very goodhearted woman.

BACHAN (*smiling*): But...

CHACHA JI (*addressing Nirmal*): But sometimes you can be gullible. Don't mind me if I say so. Sometimes you are unable to see under the surface.

NIRMAL (*amused*): Now, what did I do to prompt that?

CHACHA JI (*seriously*): Your husband, my friend since childhood, is my one and only brother. God didn't bless me with a blood brother, but he has been more than that.

NIRMAL (*to Bachan, protesting*): I don't understand. Have I wronged your friend, your brother?

CHACHA JI: Oh no, not yet. My brother, my friend here, told me that you want your son, our Roop, to marry the Captain's daughter.

NIRMAL: Nothing is arranged yet. It is an ongoing—

CHACHA JI (*interrupting Nirmal*): Yes, she is the daughter of a Captain. Yes, the family has lot of new money. Yes, the girl is convent educated. But how well do you know the Captain's wife?

NIRMAL: We went to the same college. We were not friends, but I came to know her very well.

CHACHA JI (*sipping his drink*): You knew her very well? For how long?

NIRMAL: I met her in graduate school.

CHACHA JI: That is two years. As I said, you are not a very shrewd woman; you see the good in all. Not all people are as goodhearted as you are.

BACHAN: You are not the first one to say so. This is a well-known fact. It is very easy to fool her.

NIRMAL (*flustered*): All right, all right. Nobody is trying to fool me. I still don't know where this is going.

CHACHA JI (*hurt*): It broke my heart when Bachan told me that you have almost made up your mind about the Captain's daughter.

NIRMAL: I didn't know about Preet. We have never discussed it, but in the end it is up to Roop.

CHACHA JI (*distantly*): I thought it was all settled when you came home.

NIRMAL (*as if to herself*): They were young. She was so young.

CHACHA JI (*quickly agreeing*): That is so true. I did not think that far. People do change, especially children when they grow up. You are right, Nirmal. You are absolutely right. (*He takes another sip of his drink.*) Now, our Captain Sahib, I have heard nothing but praise about him.

BACHAN: Do you know him?

CHACHA JI: I know someone who has served along with him. And when we used to live in the town, his mother and my mother came to know each other very well.

Bachan: Oh!

Chacha ji: Everyone thinks he is a man of honor and integrity.

Nirmal: They are a well-educated family.

(*Roop enters and sits at the computer table.*)

Bachan: Education! Education does not teach morality.

Chacha ji: Here, I must agree with Bachan. Education accentuates the character; whatever is there, it will come out. These days, it is a means of making a living rather than of developing character.

Nirmal: The millionaires and billionaires, they get an education. They do not need to work.

Chacha ji: They need education more than you and I do.

Roop (*intrigued*): How so, Chacha ji?

Chacha ji (*perkily*): Yes, son. They do. They need education to learn new ways to keep their wealth. Their problems are bigger than yours and mine.

Roop (*with curiosity*): How so?

CHACHA JI: For a person like me, if circumstances change, I can go and find a job, any job. Do you think they can do so? Can they do any job? No, my son, they cannot. They have not lifted a finger in their lives. Moreover, they constantly have to find new ways to hold onto that wealth. They need education to stay one step ahead of the laws and regulations.

ROOP: That makes sense.

BACHAN (*wearily*): My engineering degree was useless. Here, I could have gotten this job with a high school diploma. A useless waste of time.

CHACHA JI (*amused*): You say useless! Nirmal would not have married an uneducated boy.

BACHAN (*smiling*): You are right there. I would not have had any chance.

NIRMAL (*irked*): I married you, not your education.

CHACHA JI: Bachan, Nirmal is right. At that time, people still valued the person and the family background.

BACHAN: *Bai*, it was property and land. Since then, it is being divided down every generation.

CHACHA JI: So true.

NIRMAL: The Captain's family is very down-to-earth.

BACHAN: That is why you were trying to impress them!

NIRMAL (*annoyed*): I did no such thing.

BACHAN: You gave me ten pages of instructions on how to behave, and what to say and what not to say.

ROOP: Me too!

NIRMAL: We live in a society, not in a jungle. Sometimes, we have to do certain things.

BACHAN: But I do not understand the point of all of that when, sooner or later, the reality will come out in the end.

CHACHA JI: Bachan, the main objective behind this is that by the time the reality comes out things reach a point of no return.

ROOP: Chacha ji, these days, there is no such point.

CHACHA JI: You are right there, my son. You are right there. Times have changed.

NIRMAL: *Veer ji*, you were saying something about the Captain.

CHACHA JI: As I mentioned earlier, I have not heard anything negative about him. He is an honorable man.

BACHAN: And his wife?

CHACHA JI: I don't believe in repeating something that I have not heard with my own ears or seen with my own eyes. Nirmal knows her.

NIRMAL: As I said, I know her from graduate school. What about her?

CHACHA JI: I heard she was not very kind to the Captain's mother.

BACHAN: Oh?

NIRMAL: What happened?

CHACHA JI (*seriously*): May God forgive me if I am wrong. I didn't see anything with my own eyes or hear with my own ears. If I am wrong, I ask Almighty's forgiveness.

NIRMAL: You sound serious.

CHACHA JI (*gloomily*): Every time my mother went to visit her, she returned home grumbling and sad. The Captain had arranged for around-the-clock assistance. His mother had been sick for a long time, and to make things worse, she slipped and broke her hip and was bedridden for more than a year. Bachan, you knew my mother, she would not say anything unless it really bothered her.

BACHAN: No, I never heard anything unkind about anybody from her lips.

CHACHA JI: But we had the same cleaning woman. God forgive me, I really do not know how much truth is there. I overheard the girl telling mother that toward the end, the Captain's wife started withholding her mother-in-law's drinks and food because she kept soiling her bed.

NIRMAL (*puzzled*): Didn't you say the Captain had arranged for around-the-clock help?

CHACHA JI (*thoughtfully*): And so he did, so he did.

BACHAN: You don't withhold an old person's food because of the bed sheets.

CHACHA JI: My mother never said anything. There may not be any truth in it.

BACHAN: It wouldn't be the first time. These types of things are common.

CHACHA JI: No fear of God. He is the only one who knows the truth.

NIRMAL: But she is an educated woman.

BACHAN: What does education have to do with it?

CHACHA JI (*as if to himself*): As they say, the girls may have their fathers' personality traits, but they learn their values at their mothers' knees. They do what they see. They treat others as they see others being treated in the household.

NIRMAL (*fidgeting*): She is an educated young girl. The new generation is not like that.

BACHAN: Education! It is your heart. Where your heart is, that is what counts.

NIRMAL (*anxiously*): Ultimately, it is Roop's choice. We have promised him that we will look around, and we may suggest someone, but ultimately it is his choice. We can leave it up to Roop.

CHACHA JI (*returning to his jovial mood*): Let us leave it in God's hands. It is like old times. Bachan, sitting like this reminds me of old days. Those were good and simple times.

BACHAN: Now that we are retired, and once Roop settles down here, we can return home. We will take care of the farm. It will really be like old times.

NIRMAL (*angrily*): This is the first time I have heard about returning home.

BACHAN (*tenderly*): Why? You can live like a queen there. You could have one or two servants. You would not have to lift a finger.

NIRMAL (*suspiciously*): That was your plan all along, go back! People are running here, and you want to go back.

BACHAN: We ran here, too. That was then. Thirty years ago.

NIRMAL: More than thirty years ago. First, you left everything behind there. Now, you want to leave everything behind here.

BACHAN: What is here to leave behind?

NIRMAL: Roop, he will have his family one day. This house, our friends.

BACHAN: He will visit us as we used to visit our parents.

NIRMAL: How many times did we visit them? Those mosquitoes, and half of the day the electricity is gone.

BACHAN: I will get a generator for you.

ROOP (*gleefully*): I don't mind mosquitoes. You can use mosquito nets as we used when we visited the grandparents.

NIRMAL (*exasperated*): You and your father will never let me live in peace in one place. It is not the same back home as it was when we used to live there.

CHACHA JI: You are right, Nirmal. It is not the same. The relationships, the friends, the entire focus of life has changed. It is not the same.

NIRMAL: *Veer ji*, tell him, it is not the same.

CHACHA JI: Without a doubt, those were different times, simpler times. You can divide your time between two places. But to relocate there may be difficult.

NIRMAL (*firmly*): Tell him *Veer ji,* how difficult it would be for us. He will listen to you.

BACHAN: I am just talking casually. It is not as if I am ready to pack and leave.

CHACHA JI (*to Bachan*): For women, it is always the family ties that are so important. Naturally, Nirmal wants to stay closer to Roop. Remember when you decided to come here…*Massi ji* used to miss you very much.

BACHAN: It is not like I am moving there today. It was just a thought.

NIRMAL (*rattled*): I will not let you uproot me twice in my lifetime, especially now that the parents on both sides of the family are gone. Who is left there? I simply will not!

BACHAN: Just calm down, Nirmal.

ROOP: Mom, I do not mind settling down there and working on the farm.

NIRMAL (*torn*): All this for nothing! All this for nothing! You want to go back! Be realistic. Where will you find a job?

ROOP: I will do the farming. I will not need a job.

NIRMAL: Your father ran away from the farm, and now you want to return and play with the sand. Ask him why he ran away? He ran away. (*To Bachan*) Didn't you run away? Tell your son. Tell him, why did you run away? You had everything there.

BACHAN: Everybody was running away then. I was not the only one.

NITMAL: *Veer ji* did not. He stayed behind.

CHACHA JI (*sorrowfully*): Father passed away, and then it was too late. Times were still good back then.

NIRMAL (*pleading*): *Veer ji*, tell them. Tell them *Veer ji*, to wake up from their dream world. Tell them about the corruption. Tell Roop how difficult it is to get things done there.

CHACHA JI: Son, life can get tough there. Things do not move there as smoothly as you are used to here. For a common man, things can be tough, especially if you do not know anyone. You have to know the right people in the right places.

NIRMAL (*feeling agitated*): Going back! One thing after another; there is no peace for me.

BACHAN (*tenderly*): I did not mean to upset you. We were just talking causally.

NIRMAL (*indignantly*): There is no casual talk with you, is there? In 1972, you got your passport and ticket before you let anyone in on your plan. Your parents, my parents, we were all shocked.

CHACHA JI (*surprised*): He did not tell anyone?

BACHAN (*to Chacha ji*): You were the first to know. (*To Nirmal*) We are not going anywhere. I am sorry. I did not mean to upset you.

NIRMAL: Everything is a joke to you. Let me be clear. This time, you will be going alone.

(*Roop whispers in Nirmal's ear. She nods her head, and Roop returns to his seat.*)

BACHAN (*to Chacha ji, smiling*): *Bai*, then, it will be just like old times, you and me.

CHACHA JI (*amused*): It won't be a pretty sight, two old codgers sitting there under the *pippal* tree. Do not worry, Nirmal. He is not going anywhere. He is just being emotional about home. He is not going anywhere.

NIRMAL: He is an obstinate man.

CHACHA JI (*smiling*): So he is. But he is always obstinate about doing the right thing, and the right thing is to keep you happy.

BACHAN (*to Nirmal*): It would not be the same without you. (*The doorbell rings. Roop exits.*) Who can that be at this hour?

NIRMAL (*looking at Bachan*): Roop ordered dinner.

CHACHA JI: Now, that was very thoughtful of Roop. (*To Nirmal*) You have raised a good son. That is all that counts, raising good, kind-hearted, and honest children. As mother used to say, that is all we are leaving behind. Both of you should be proud of yourselves.

BACHAN: He turned out to be a good young man with the grace of God. Nirmal raised him well.

(*Roop returns with boxes and plates. As they are getting ready to eat, the lights dim.*)

*Curtain.*

# SCENE SIX

*Late Sunday afternoon. Bachan, Roop, Nirmal, and Chacha ji enter the family room one by one. As they are taking off their coats, Roop collects them. Roop exits with the coats. As they are seating themselves, Roop returns.*

CHACHA JI: What a beautiful and spacious temple. Quite a gathering!

ROOP: Chacha ji, the one on the east side is even more spacious.

BACHAN: Our people are good at raising temples on every corner.

NIRMAL: What is wrong with that?

BACHAN: Nirmal! Nothing is wrong with building temples. But what is wrong is erasing the history of our people, especially our religion.

NIRMAL: People are becoming more religious than before.

BACHAN: For example, where is the Wall? Marble is everywhere, where is the Wall? What is happening to our historical sites and other artifacts?

ROOP: What Wall?

BACHAN: The two sons of our tenth Guru Gobind Singh Ji; nine year-old Zorawar Singh and seven year-old Fateh Singh, were bricked up alive within a wall when they refused to convert to Islam.

ROOP: Whoever is responsible for that destruction should be tried as a criminal.

NIRMAL (*nervously*): Do not give him any ideas. It is not safe to talk about these things these days.

CHACHA JI: All people but ours cherish their history.

NIRMAL: *Veer ji*, that is all they talk about in temples, nothing but history.

BACHAN: The only history they talk about is to instigate and fool people.

CHACHA JI: Other people know how to preserve their history. The museums are full of artifacts: the pebbles, centuries old torn clothes, torn and crumbled papers—

BACHAN: It is our own people. No one has to do us harm. We are destroying ourselves.

ROOP: Their DNA must be on the bricks!

CHACHA JI (*intensely*): What an intelligent observation! My son, I never thought about it that far.

ROOP: As I said, they should be tried as criminals.

NIRMAL (*reproachfully*): Look what you two have done. (*To Roop, beseechingly*) You must keep your opinions to yourself. You listen to me, son. Keep these opinions to yourself.

BACHAN: It is a crime! Is it not? It is.

NIRMAL (*irritated*): You two, be quiet. Talk about something else.

BACHAN: We are having a friendly, casual discussion.

NIRMAL (*distressed*): There is no casual discussion with you. There is nothing casual with this type of talk. Do not put ideas in his head. You know how he likes to argue.

BACHAN: Nothing is wrong in expressing one's opinions.

NIRMAL (*exasperated*): Plenty is wrong. It is not a matter of a right or wrong opinion. It is where you are expressing it, in whose company you are expressing your opinions. Just leave it alone, you two. Leave it alone.

BACHAN: *Hadd kar ti*[16], Nirmal! We cannot discuss this within our own four walls?

NIRMAL (*worried*): You know very well how eager these children are to express their opinions regardless of the company. These days it is not safe.

CHACHA JI: Bachan, Nirmal is right to be cautious. We live in different times.

ROOP (*assuring*): Don't worry, Mom. I am not that careless.

NIRMAL: Not too careful. This topic should not be discussed outside our home. (*To Roop*) You swear by me that you will never discuss this outside these walls, son.

ROOP: Don't worry, Mom.

CHACHA JI: Our Roop has a good head on his shoulders.

NIRMAL (*tensely*): You don't know *Veer ji*. These children here are too quick to express their views.

BACHAN: You cannot live in fear.

NIRMAL (*troubled*): What is the use of useless talk?

---

16 **hadd kar ti**. For crying out loud, for God's sake, for goodness's sake.

BACHAN: It is not useless; it is merely a discussion. We are not starting a new movement. It is only a casual discussion.

NIRMAL: Casual? There is nothing casual about it.

ROOP: Mom, please don't worry. We are just discussing a few facts. We are not naming any names. It is not the first time. My friends and I, we have the same concerns. That is why we think we will have our own temples where we will be able to take our families. Keep it simple, based on teachings of Guru Nanak[17]. We do talk about these things among ourselves.

NIRMAL (*nervously*): What was I saying? Was I not right? No peace for me, no peace! This is the first time I am hearing about this.

ROOP: Mom, most of the time, we do not know what they are talking about in temple, but the teachings are pretty simple: live a truthful life, work hard, and do *sewa*[18], which is all relatable. It is not complicated, Mom.

NIRMAL (*as if to herself*): There is much I do not know. What is going on around me? Where did I go wrong?

---

17 ***Guru Nanak***. Founder of the religion of Sikhism and is the first of the Sikh Gurus.
18 ***sewa***. Charitable service.

BACHAN: Nirmal, you are becoming anxious for nothing. Look how sensible these young people are!

CHACHA JI: We live in different times. Nirmal is right in saying one has to be careful.

BACHAN: Our Roop is a very wise young man. Son, as they say of politics and religion: stay away from them. No one wins those arguments.

ROOP: There is too much emphasis on outward appearance.

CHACHA JI (*firmly*): Neither does *janeu* make a Brahmin, nor does baptism make a true Sikh. (*To Roop*) As you said, our gurus have left us with the tradition of *sewa* and leading a life of truth and hard work.

ROOP: What is *janeu*?

CHACHA JI: It is a sacred thread that Brahmins wear.

NIRMAL (*perplexed*): How can you compare it? How can you say that? It is part of our religion. You cannot dismiss *rehat-mriada*[19] due to the actions of a few.

---

19 **rehat-mriada**. Way of life.

BACHAN: Nirmal, it is part…an important part…but look around you and see what is happening in our temples.

CHACHA JI (*in a conciliatory manner*): No, do not get me wrong. I am all for *janeu* and baptism, but one should not hide behind them and claim to be pious.

ROOP: I personally think one should lead an exemplary life first to be worthy of baptism.

CHACHA JI (*with enthusiasm*): Now, my son, this is a very wise observation. I completely agree with you.

NIRMAL (*with concern*): *Veer ji*, do not encourage him. It is not safe to be so vocal about these things nowadays.

CHACHA JI: Nirmal, I am not attacking anything whatsoever. What I am saying is as a *janeu* does not make a Brahmin, so baptism does not make a man pious, a true Sikh. I am just referring to what is going on around us.

BACHAN: *Bai* is right, but divisiveness—the greed, the corruption—is pervasive in all aspects of society. It is unavoidable. Sooner or later, some of it is bound to seep into religious institutions.

CHACHA JI: The religious institutions and the priests should be the beacons of honesty and goodness; a place people can go and seek help in times of need.

ROOP: They just recite prayers, and when you try to listen, there is somebody sitting next to you whispering the prayers along with the priest. What I say is this: if you want to do that, stay home and let others try to listen. Besides reading the scriptures, Mom, what else—

CHACHA JI (*with enthusiasm*): Nirmal, how perceptive! How perceptive this young man is! Roop, that is all they do because that is all they are trained to do.

NIRMAL: That is the only requirement.

BACHAN: That is the problem. That is the only requirement. As long as someone can read the scriptures and keep up with the outside—

NIRMAL: They are doing a good job. In foreign countries, they assist you with the rituals from birth to death. They are there for us. They are the center of the community.

CHACHA JI: So they do, especially the ones who carry on day-to-day sevices. They are good organizers and put forth effort above and beyond the call of duty.

NIRMAL: They are there in good times as well as bad times.

ROOP: To read the scriptures!

NIRMAL (*annoyed*): What is wrong with that?

BACHAN: They interpret and focus on what they want and what serves their purpose.

ROOP: Other traditions have highly educated priests, and they do more than just read the scriptures. People can go to them for counseling and guidance.

BACHAN: That part, I am not sure.

NIRMAL: What part?

BACHAN: Guidance and counseling.

NIRMAL: Sometimes you just want to talk to someone. I think it can be good, especially when you are so far away from your family. You know how it is; you cannot discuss anything with anybody. If you do, it is all over town by the end of the day.

BACHAN: Why would you want to talk to the priest, a stranger? Talk to your family.

NIRMAL (*on edge*): When family is the problem!

BACHAN: So, your family—

NIRMAL (*stiffly*): Do not be so sensitive. You know what I mean.

ROOP: Dad, Mom has a point.

NIRMAL: Especially for women, there is no place to go.

ROOP: They should be able to provide needed counsel or, at least, another ear if you need to get something off your chest.

BACHAN: That is what friends are for, not priests.

CHACHA JI: You better choose your friends wisely unless you want to spread your inner most feelings all over the city, as Nirmal said.

ROOP: Chacha ji, nowadays, phones ring right away and e-mails are sent right away unless one has a friend like Mom. She is on the phone listening to other people for hours at a time.

NIRMAL: I do not want to be rude. I do not lose anything if I listen or if I can be of some help. Some of these young girls are so far away from home for the first time in their lives.

ROOP: Mom, you tend to overdo it, and you get stressed out yourself.

NIRMAL: I do not get stressed out. You and your dad become restless when I am on the phone.

ROOP: Mom, you are on the phone for hours at a time.

BACHAN: They keep her entertained.

NIRMAL: Everything is a joke to you. Other people's problems are entertainment for you!

BACHAN (*to Nirmal*): If our priests start listening to people's problems, what will you do?

CHACHA JI: Besides reading scriptures, these people are not equipped to advise anyone on anything.

BACHAN: They do not have the education or training. They are not aware of the stresses and strains of life here. (*To Nirmal, affectionately*) And you can always talk to me. I am a good listener.

NIRMAL: When have you ever heard me calling someone on the phone to pour my heart out? Even if there was something like that available, I would not go to them.

BACHAN (*in a conciliatory tone*): That much I must say, Roop. Your mother never discusses or complains about family matters outside the house; not that she has anything to complain about!

NIRMAL: That is what you think!

BACHAN: What do you mean?

NIRMAL: There were times—

BACHAN: This is the first I am hearing of them.

NIRMAL (*irritated*): What are you hearing? I have not said anything yet. It was not easy to be so far away from my family with no shoulder to cry on.

BACHAN (*puzzled*): Cry? Cry about what?

NIRMAL (*angrily*): Cry about what? You were away from the house for twelve hours at a time. I was sitting alone with a child, no friends, and no family.

BACHAN (*tenderly*): I didn't know you were so unhappy. Why didn't you—

NIRMAL (*warily*): It had nothing to do with you.

BACHAN: But—

NIRMAL (*agitated*): Do not be so sensitive. It had nothing to do with you.

ROOP: Dad, Mom must have felt lonely and trapped here.

BACHAN (*perplexed*): Trapped?

NIRMAL (*uneasily*): It is all in the past.

BACHAN (*as if to himself*): Trapped?

NIRMAL: As I said, it had nothing to do with you.

BACHAN: This is the first I am hearing about it.

NIRMAL: It was my problem, not yours.

BACHAN (*self-consciously*): What did I do?

NIRMAL: Work.

BACHAN: Work?

NIRMAL: It was my problem, not yours.

BACHAN (*nodding his head, taking a deep breath*): Trapped?

ROOP: Dad, why are you so surprised? You were at work. You worked long hours and irregular shifts; mom must have missed her family.

CHACHA JI (*to Roop*): You are wise beyond your years, my son.

NIRMAL (*to Bachan*): It was not your fault. That was the way things were then.

BACHAN (*dismayed, as if talking to himself*): Sometimes I wonder, was it all worth it?

NIRMAL (*serenely, stroking Roop's arm*): It was all worth it. Yes, it was. It has to be. It will be.

(*The lights are dimmed.*)

*Curtain.*

# SCENE SEVEN

*The following week. Break room in the campus cafeteria. Preet is sitting with her belongings scattered on the table. She is busy with her papers. Roop enters hastily.*

---

ROOP: Hello there.

PREET (*surprised, looking up*): Hello.

(*Roop points toward the empty chair. Preet nods and collects her belongings from that side of the table.*)

ROOP: The other day, you forgot my phone number.

PREET: I was looking for it. It must have slipped out of my notebook.

ROOP: You were looking for it! (*With concern*) Is something the matter?

PREET: Oh no! (*Abruptly*) What are you doing here?

ROOP: Filling out some forms.

PREET: Looking for a job?

ROOP: Oh, yes, I have been to a few interviews already.

PREET (*playfully*): It seems like things are moving along for you. What about on the home front?

ROOP: What do you mean?

PREET: Have you decided to get married to the girl your parents chose for you?

ROOP: There has been a new development.

PREET (*intrigued*): Oh, yes?

ROOP: My father's childhood friend, more than his friend as he puts it, has a daughter. I call him Cha-cha ji, not that he is my real uncle or anything like that. Apparently, back home on your father's side of the family, anyone who is younger than your father is *Chacha ji* and anyone who is older than your father is *Taia ji*. Well, (*shrugs embarrassingly*) you know all that. So, this Chacha ji also has a daughter. My dad is close to this guy. From their conversations, they are more like brothers, very close.

PREET (*brightly*): So, there is competition.

ROOP: As long as they are dealing with it, I have some breathing room.

(*There is a pause.*)

PREET: What do you think?

ROOP: I have not seen the other girl. She came here recently.

PREET: Oh!

ROOP: And my mom says it takes time to break in a new person. It takes time for them to become accustomed to the new culture here.

PREET (*amused*): It sounds like breaking in a new pair of shoes.

ROOP: She likes the other girl.

PREET: Has she seen the new arrival?

ROOP: No, not recently. But look at you, you don't need any—

PREET: Breaking in?

ROOP (*protesting*): Well, don't put it that way. You came recently. You seem to be at home here. I wouldn't have known if you had not told me.

PREET: Yes?

ROOP (*looking away*): My mom, she has this idea of sophistication in her mind, a convent-educated daughter of this military officer. Her mind is full of these sorts of things.

PREET: And the other girl?

ROOP: She is the daughter of my father's friend from our village. All her life she studied in boarding schools. But, my mom... (*He shakes his head.*)

PREET: What do you think?

ROOP (*ambivalent*): I do not know what to think.

PREET: You know her father, but you don't know her. That is a problem.

ROOP (*uneasily*): The entire situation is unexplainable. I like him very much. It is easy and fun to be around him. But—

PREET: But you don't know the daughter. You are thinking what sort of girl she might be. Would she hold a candle to the Captain's daughter? I get the picture.

ROOP: So, you do understand, don't you?

PREET (*smiling*): Of course, I do. You want to examine all your options.

ROOP: Yes, yes, all options. But I don't want to hurt Chacha ji's feelings.

PREET: Feelings?

ROOP: Chacha ji's feelings.

PREET: Oh, yes, of course.

ROOP: She will be going to college here.

PREET: Here?

ROOP: That is what Chacha ji said. I wish I could know who she is without her knowing.

PREET (*interested*): You mean to say, you want to see her without her knowing it. It certainly would make your choice easy.

ROOP: If I don't like her, then I could go with Mom's choice.

PREET: Why don't you ask your Chacha ji to show you her picture?

ROOP: It would seem odd.

PREET: No, it wouldn't. (*Firmly*) He should not expect you to marry his daughter without you first seeing her. He can't be that irrational!

ROOP: He thinks I have seen her already.

PREET: You have?

ROOP: Now, he is being irrational in some ways. I saw her only once when we were children. People do change. She might turn out to be an ill-mannered brat since she is an only child, or she might be a sophisticated, caring, and well-mannered young lady. (*With emphasis*) I do like Chacha ji. He is open and straightforward. I feel good when he is around...like family.

PREET: How about the other family?

ROOP: I do not know them that well. They were trying to impress us, and my mom was trying to impress them. (*Amused*) My dad and I were looking at each other. It was a day full of commotion.

PREET: So, were you impressed?

ROOP: I am a simple person. I do not need any impressing.

PREET: You don't seem that simple to me. (*She resumes rearranging her belongings. Firmly*) I wish I could help you, but this is a maze you have to walk out of yourself.

ROOP: You can help me.

PREET (*puzzled*): I can?

(*He writes down the phone number and hands her the slip of paper.*)

ROOP: First, here is my number. Do not drop it this time!

(*Preet takes the paper, folds it, and puts in her purse.*)

ROOP (*hesitantly*): Are you sure you don't mind?

PREET: But I don't know what I can do for you?

ROOP: Oh, there is. There is something you can do for me.

PREET (*baffled*): I don't understand. How I can be of help to you? You don't want me to do something illegal, do you?

ROOP (*feeling self-conscious*): Oh, nothing like that.

PREET: Spy for you? Pretend to be your girlfriend?

ROOP (*smiling*): Now, there is an idea! Both parties will run away, and my parents will throw me out in no time.

PREET (*surprised*): Because you have a girlfriend?

ROOP: Because I did not tell them. My mom has asked me many times. Now all of a sudden—

PREET: What do you care? You already have job offers.

ROOP: No! No, it is nothing like that.

PREET (*curiously*): Then what?

ROOP (*seriously*): Once classes start, you will be coming to campus regularly. (*Preet nods*) Well, (*uneasily*) well, if I show you an old picture of her, even though she was in eighth or ninth grade, if you see any resemblance at all…you girls are good at that sort of thing. Even if you're not sure she is the same person, please call me.

PREET (*perplexed*): Call you! Call you for what?

ROOP (*flustered*): So that I can see her without her father knowing about it.

PREET: And if you don't like her, you can go along with your mom's choice.

ROOP: And if I like her, I will ask my dad to convince my mom.

PREET (*astonished*): Once more, what do you want me to do? Look for that girl? As I understand, you will be here throughout this semester. Why don't you do it yourself?

ROOP (*uneasily*): I will. I will, too. But the picture is too old. I won't know even if she passes right in front of me. You girls have that sixth sense. You will know.

PREET (*as if to herself*): If we girls have that sixth sense, we would raise…oh, never mind.

ROOP (*earnestly*): Just in case you come across her, or someone with a little resemblance, please call me.

PREET: Sure, I will.

ROOP (*calmly*): It is so easy to talk to you, from the first day we met. Are you sure we have never met before? Of course not!

PREET: Where is the picture?

ROOP (*takes out the picture from his wallet and hands over to Preet*): See how old and faded it is? See for yourself.

(*Preet looks at the picture intently. Suddenly, she is unsettled. She looks at the picture then at Roop. She tries to collect herself.*)

PREET: It is faded. Is that you?

ROOP (*nervously*): Yes, yes that is me. Can't you tell?

PREET (*distracted*): As you said, it is old and you were young. It is difficult to say.

ROOP (*self-consciously*): I still look the same, don't you think? Older but the same. She was too young. I am sure she looks different now.

PREET (*trying to hide her anger*): Too young, you say. How young? She looks grown-up to me.

ROOP: As I said, it is difficult with the girls. They change so much.

PREET (*rebounding*): They do change, don't they?

ROOP: You agree with me. It is so easy to talk to you.

PREET: I agree with you that she seems too simple; she's no match for the convent-educated girl.

ROOP: I won't know until I see her.

PREET: She looks like a simpleton to me.

ROOP: Does she?

PREET: Can't you tell from this picture?

ROOP: Can you?

(*He tries to look at the picture. Preet turns it toward him. He examines it intently as if looking at it for the first time. Preet, hastily takes the picture away from him.*)

PREET: Look at her hair. Two long loops hanging on her shoulders like ropes. And this frock! It is way too long. She must have borrowed it from someone.

ROOP: That was the fashion then.

PREET (*irked*): So, you do remember the fashion then?

ROOP (*awkwardly*): Well—

PREET: Fashion or no fashion, she is too simple for you. Don't you think?

(*Roop tries to look at the picture, but Preet quickly takes it away.*)

ROOP: You think so?

PREET (*sarcastically*): You should know one thing about village people.

ROOP: What?

PREET: That they don't change that easily.

ROOP (*seriously*): They don't?

(*Preet nods.*)

PREET (*bitterly*): You can't compare a convent-educated girl to her. She is plain.

(*Preet holds the picture in front of her. Roop tries to look at it, but she takes it away quickly.*)

ROOP: She might have changed by now.

PREET: Village people! Oh no. No manners! No table manners! No fashion sense!

ROOP (*feeling uncomfortable*): No?

PREET: You better give it serious thought.

ROOP (*torn*): But, but I like him.

PREET: But you won't be living with him. Will you? (*Pointing at the picture*) It is her that you should be concerned about.

ROOP (*ambivalent*): You are right! She may not be able to adjust in this culture.

PREET: A girl from a village! How can she?

ROOP: You are right. How can she?

(*There is a pause.*)

PREET (*quickly*): What if she turns out to be just like me? Right off the plane?

ROOP (*amused*): If she turns out to be like you, then…well then, my father will have to convince my mom.

PREET: Why?

ROOP: Because—

PREET (*looking at her phone*): Excuse me. It is my father. (*She answers the phone. She carefully places the picture in her purse.*) What do you know? We are going to a function. They are already outside waiting for me in the car. (*She hastily collects her belongings.*)

ROOP: Function?

PREET (*agitated*): Some birthday party? I hate these parties. I don't know why he has to drag me with him.

ROOP (*softly*): I thought all girls like parties.

PREET: I don't mind when I know the people.

ROOP: My mom likes parties. Every week, Dad and I used to resist, but now we just go along. After a while, you get used to them. You will be fine.

PREET (*getting up*): I don't know.

ROOP (*pushes his chair aside as Preet is leaving and tries to assist her with her belongings, softly*): Remember your assignment.

PREET (*taken aback*): My assignment! Yes, my assignment! (*She is exasperated but trying to control herself. While leaving, as if to herself*) You may have your answer sooner than you think.

ROOP: What did you say?

PREET (*turning around*): I said bye.

(*Preet exits hurriedly.*)

ROOP (*hesitantly*): Bye! (*Whispering to himself*) And what is your name? (*Feeling dejected, he returns to his seat and slowly slides down in the chair.*)

*Curtain.*

# SCENE EIGHT

*A secluded room at the party hall complex. The room has decorative flowers and some furniture. There is a window along the back wall and entrance doors on both side walls. In the background, music is playing.*

*Chacha ji is sitting on a chair. Preet strolls in.*

---

PREET: Here you are, Father. You left me there all alone.

CHACHA JI: I just came in a minute ago.

(*Roop rushes in.*)

ROOP (*addressing Preet*): I need to talk to you. Oh, I didn't see you, Chacha ji. Excuse me.

CHACHA JI (*surprised*): You have met!

PREET (*addressing Chacha ji*): Yes, we have. (*To Roop, annoyed*) And I have nothing to say to you.

ROOP: I just want to explain.

PREET: There is nothing to explain.

ROOP (*earnestly*): I didn't know.

PREET (*stiffly*): Now, you know.

ROOP: I didn't realize until you got to the party.

PREET: Well, now you know. Father, he called you a dictator.

CHACHA JI: He did?

ROOP: She was complaining that she was brought here against her wishes.

PREET: That is no secret. He knows how I feel. Don't you Father?

ROOP: She had tears in her eyes.

CHACHA JI: She did?

PREET: He also called you a tyrant.

CHACHA JI: He did?

ROOP: I thought she was brought here against her wishes.

PREET: I was. He knows. It is no secret.

ROOP: Well, I felt—

PREET: He also wanted me to spy for him.

ROOP (*uneasily*): Spying? It was not spying.

CHACHA JI (*perplexed*): Spying?

ROOP (*helplessly*): It was not spying, Chacha ji.

PREET: He wanted me to find this girl.

CHACHA JI: A girl, why?

PREET: So he could compare her to some officer's daughter.

CHACHA JI (*unsettled*): Some officer's daughter. Compare? And you know who that girl is?

ROOP: Chacha ji, she called you stubborn.

CHACHA JI: Did she?

PREET: I make no secret of it.

ROOP: She also called you mule headed.

CHACHA JI: Did she?

PREET: Again, no secret there.

CHACHA JI (*amused*): I believe you there. She might have called me that. My mother used to call me mule headed. Preet picked it up from my mother. May God rest her soul. (*In a serious tone*) The boy I carried on my shoulders at the farm so he would not get a splinter in his foot calls me a dictator. What is happening to this world?

ROOP: No, Chacha ji, it was not like that.

CHACHA JI (*disappointed*): Every time you came to visit, I loved you like the son I never had, and you call me a tyrant.

ROOP (*flustered*): No, Chacha ji, it was not like that.

CHACHA JI (*disheartened*): I thought you might have a soft heart like your father; a generous soul like your father who is no less than my brother, my dear childhood friend. Preet has reason. I will be leaving her thousands of miles away. Only God knows how it is breaking my heart. She has good reason, but, son, I have given you no such reason.

ROOP (*tensely*): It is not—

CHACHA JI (*looking at Preet who is looking outside the window*): Didn't I tell you? Let us wait and see. (*Dryly*)

People change. (*To Roop*) You have changed the blood that runs in my friend's veins, son. (*He wipes his forehead with the handkerchief.*)

Roop (*earnestly*): But it is not…please let me explain.

Chacha ji (*annoyed*): Explain! There is no need to explain.

(*Preet is still looking through the window. Nirmal is at the door entrance. She does not see Preet and Chacha ji.*)

Nirmal (*hastily*): Roop, where are you? Captain Sahib is waiting for you. Come on, son.

(*Roop hesitantly follows Nirmal and exits. Chacha ji slowly walks over and sits down. Preet follows him.*)

Preet: Father, you want me to stay amid these people, so far away from you?

Chacha ji (*gloomily*): Maybe I have been wrong.

Preet (*quietly*): Let me return home with you, Father.

Chacha ji: But you have joined the university already.

Preet: But there are universities at home as well.

CHACHA JI: It is only for two years. It will be good for the rest of your life.

PREET (*unhappily*): Two years can be long time. Father, what if something happens to you? I will be so far away.

CHACHA JI (*reassuringly*): Nothing will happen to me. I am as healthy as a horse.

PREET (*distantly*): Father, haven't I been a good girl?

CHACHA JI (*tenderly*): Yes, you have been. I could not have asked for a better daughter.

PREET: Haven't I done whatever you have asked me to do?

CHACHA JI: Yes, you have.

PREET (*pleading*): Let me come with you. Let me stay with you. Let me be with you when—

CHACHA JI: But I wish to see you settled in your house, with your own family.

PREET: You are my family. Father, don't push me so far away.

CHACHA JI (*warmly*): Oh, you don't understand, daughter. This is the way it is. Even if you come home now, I can't keep you in my house forever. Sooner or later, you have to build your own life.

PREET: But, Father. (*She kneels beside him.*)

CHACHA JI: Sh, sh. (*He strokes her head.*) Things will work out. God is always watching over you. Every six months, you will come home or I will come here. I will call you every week.

PREET: Every week!

CHACHA JI: Every day. Two years will fly by in no time. Then—

PREET (*with renewed liveliness*): Then, I will come home and stay with you.

CHACHA JI (*assuring her*): Yes, of course. (*He pauses*) People sure change with time, don't they? How foolish to think that so and so's son or daughter will be just like them. An old way of thinking, isn't it?

PREET: Yes, Father.

CHACHA JI: Yes, it is a foolish way, but are you not just like me? You are mule headed, stubborn, and can be a little dictator. Just like me.

PREET: Oh, Father, you are just impossible, and you mustn't be so harsh on Roop. He was trying to be sympathetic toward me. He didn't know I was your daughter.

CHACHA JI: But still, I have my doubts now.

PREET: Oh, Father, you are too harsh.

(*Chacha ji and Preet exit. Roop enters.*)

ROOP (*distracted*): They are gone. She is gone.

(*Nirmal rushes in behind Roop.*)

NIRMAL: Who is gone?

ROOP: Oh! Mother, my life is finished.

NIRMAL (*puzzled*): Don't be so dramatic. Who is gone?

ROOP: Never mind, Mother. Never mind. I will find her. I will. I must.

NIRMAL: Who?

ROOP (*restlessly*): Leave me alone, Mother.

NIRMAL: What did I do?

ROOP (*indifferently*): Nothing, Mother. I need time. I need time.

NIRMAL (*irked*): Time for what?

ROOP: Time to settle down.

NIRMAL: You will get married and settle down.

ROOP (*firmly*): No, Mother! I need time, time to…time to find a job, be on my own, and then get married.

NIRMAL: Until then, both of you can stay with us.

ROOP: No, Mother. I want to stand on my own two feet…

NIRMAL: Of course, you want to do that. You want to be responsible.

ROOP: Yes, yes. I need time, Mother.

NIRMAL: Good relationships do not come your way all the time, and Captain Sahib has to return home next month.

ROOP (*apathetically*): He can go back. I am not holding him back.

NIRMAL: His family wants a marriage ceremony before he leaves.

ROOP: Mother, I have met the girl only once, and that was while all of you were around. I do not know her.

NIRMAL: Go to the movies. Take her to lunch or dinner. She is a very friendly, and outgoing girl.

ROOP: Mother, that's not what I mean. Going to the movies…what would that do? I don't know her.

NIRMAL: I am telling you. Trust me. She is a charming, pleasant girl.

ROOP: Mother, you promised me that you wouldn't force me.

NIRMAL: But Captain Sahib has to return to attend to an urgent business matter.

ROOP (*on edge*): More urgent than his daughter's marriage?

NIRMAL (*exasperated*): Now, you are just being difficult.

(*Neetu enters.*)

NEETU (*to Roop, gaily*): I have been looking all over for you.

ROOP (*uneasily*): Sorry.

NIRMAL: Go son. Go with her.

(*Roop hesitantly leaves with Neetu. Bachan enters.*)

NIRMAL (*wringing her hands and pacing*): Your son!

BACHAN (*perplexed*): My son?

NIRMAL: Yes, your son!

BACHAN (*amused*): Yes, what has my son done?

NIRMAL: Oh, I can't show my face now. How can I show my face?

BACHAN (*smiling*): I am looking at your face. Nothing is wrong with it.

NIRMAL: Oh, stop it! Stop it!

BACHAN (*tenderly*): What is the matter?

NIRMAL: He says he needs more time.

BACHAN: Who needs more time?

NIRMAL: Your son!

BACHAN: Time for what?

NIRMAL: To settle down, to find a job.

BACHAN (*calmly*): He has a point there. He wants to find a job so he can take care of his responsibilities. What is wrong with that?

NIRMAL: I told him that until then, both of them can stay with us.

BACHAN: If he wants to start his life his way, let him. It will be good for us. (*Affectionately*) Just you and me… the way we started our lives.

NIRMAL (*annoyed*): Stop it. Just you and me…what would we do?

BACHAN: Plenty.

NIRMAL: Oh, just stop it. Everything is falling apart. All I have done for that boy, your son! Everything is falling apart. They will leave. The Captain wants to return home.

BACHAN: If our boy is not worth waiting for, then let them go.

NIRMAL: Go! Go! You say go! A convent-educated girl. A Captain's daughter. You say let it go. She has a house in her name on an acre of land in the middle of the city. Prime property, and you say let it go!

BACHAN (*steadily*): What does it matter to us what she has in her name? Our son has a house, our house. We have land. There is no competition here. Don't get blinded by all this.

NIRMAL (*anxiously*): But they want an answer, yes or no?

BACHAN: Yes or no! We are not exchanging pieces of property. Yes or no!

NIRMAL: Impossible! Impossible! They want to settle down their daughter. I don't blame them. If they detect hesitation on our part, they may find another suitable boy. There are plenty of them around here.

BACHAN: Then, let them.

NIRMAL (*bitterly*): That is what you want, don't you? From the beginning, you did not support me. You want that village girl for your son, don't you?

BACHAN (*confused*): How can you say that? I have been with you all the way. How can you say such things?

I do support you. (*He pauses*) I have not seen that girl since she was this tall. (*He gestures with his hand.*)

NIRMAL (*dejected*): Everything I worked for day and night: fed him, took care of him, raised him, and educated him. Now I am trying to find a suitable match for him. I am so tired. Nobody listens. I give up. I give up.

BACHAN (*smiling*): I agree you did most of the work. But he studied, he worked hard, and he loves you. He has brought a good name to the family. This time, maybe we should give him some space. Otherwise, we may end up regretting it.

NIRMAL (*as if to herself*): I am already regretting it, all the effort I put into it. All for nothing.

(*Neetu and Roop return.*)

NEETU (*gaily*): Auntie, Mom wants to talk to you.

(*Nirmal and Neetu exit.*)

ROOP: Mom seems upset.

BACHAN: She will be all right.

ROOP: Look, Dad!

BACHAN: Your mother told me that you want time. That is fine. But we must say yes or no to these people. These are honorable people. We cannot keep them dangling in the air without an answer.

ROOP (*restlessly*): Yes, Dad. But—

BACHAN: Is there another girl?

ROOP: I don't know?

BACHAN: That is the strangest answer I have ever heard.

ROOP: I mean yes and no.

BACHAN: You don't like the Captain's daughter!

ROOP: What is there not to like, Dad? But…

BACHAN: So, there is another girl.

ROOP: Yes…yes…but I don't know…if she…

BACHAN: Who is she?

ROOP: I would rather not say.

(*Chacha ji enters.*)

CHACHA JI: It is quite a party. The band, the food…a nice arrangement. An elegant banquet hall.

BACHAN: Yes. You didn't bring Preet with you?

CHACHA JI: She is in the hall. Sometimes the world can be so small. She met a girl from her high school. (*Preet enters*) Here she is. Your uncle was just asking about you.

(*Preet presses her palms together and bows her head slightly.*)

BACHAN: How grown-up you are! When I last saw you, you were this tall. (*He signs with his hand*) This is my son, Roop.

PREET (*hesitantly, in a low voice to Roop*): Hi.

ROOP: Dad, I better go and talk to Mom.

BACHAN: Don't worry. She will be fine. (*To Chacha ji*) His mother is annoyed with him.

CHACHA JI: Why son? You must have hurt your mother's feelings.

(*Nirmal enters.*)

NIRMAL (*agitated*): They are gone…they are gone…
when I told him…he says he needs time…time for
what? That's what he said…they are gone…your son
has ruined me…I can't show my face now…how can
I? They said call us—call them and say what? I can't
show my face now.

BACHAN: He didn't run away. He is standing right here.
Your reputation is intact.

(*Preet is standing near the window during the
conversation.*)

BACHAN: Look who is here, that little girl with pony-
tails. She is all grown-up.

(*Preet comes toward Nirmal and presses her palms
together.*)

NIRMAL: Oh! (*First, she looks at Chacha ji and
then at Preet*) Oh! My God, she is. Isn't she all
grown-up? Come daughter…come sit down…
maybe you can put some sense into his head…he
is walking away…he is pushing away a good family…a Captain's covenant-educated daughter. You
seem like a sensible girl. Put some sense into him,
you must…

CHACHA JI: We must go. My sister-in-law is waiting for us. Roop, son, would you call a taxi for us?

ROOP: Please don't go yet. Stay for a few minutes. I will drop you later.

BACHAN: Why don't you stay with us today?

CHACHA JI: Preet wants to spend some time with her aunt and her cousins before the classes start.

ROOP (*looking at Preet*): But, I must...

NIRMAL: Daughter, for my sake, put some sense into my boy. He shouldn't throw away his life...I have worked so hard for him.

CHACHA JI : We must take our leave for now. Roop, son, please call a taxi for us.

(*Roop steps toward the window, and calls for the taxi using his cell phone. Occasionally, he looks out through the window.*)

NIRMAL (*holding Preet's hand*): Promise me, daughter. You will talk to him. He can be stubborn sometimes, but he is a good boy.

PREET (*looking at her father*): Aren't they all?

NIRMAL: What?

PREET: Stubborn?

NIRMAL: Yes! Yes! They are. They all can be, yes. Yes, you seem like a sensible girl. Yes, they can be stubborn. They don't know what they put us through.

(*Bachan and Chacha ji are looking at each other. Roop is looking through the window.*)

ROOP: Chacha ji, your taxi is here.

NIRMAL (*squeezing Preet's hand*): Daughter, you must talk some sense into him. You must come and visit us sometime.

PREET (*uneasily*): Yes, Auntie.

ROOP: But, I must… (*He hesitantly steps toward Preet as she is leaving.*)

(*Chacha ji takes Preet's arm, hastily bids them good bye, and exits.*)

*Curtain.*

# SCENE NINE

*One week later, Bachan and Roop are sitting in the campus cafeteria. Roop is facing the entrance door and Bachan has his back to the entrance.*

BACHAN: Why did you bring me here?

ROOP (*urgently*): We need to talk, Dad. It is about Chacha ji.

BACHAN (*smiling*): That little ponytailed girl has surely grown up.

ROOP (*uneasily*): She has, Dad. She has!

BACHAN: He is very proud of her. He did good job bringing up that little girl without a mother. I don't think I could have done that.

ROOP: Sure, Dad. You would have done so too. This is where I met her.

BACHAN: Met who?

ROOP: Chacha ji's daughter.

BACHAN: Oh!

ROOP: But I did not know she was his daughter.

BACHAN: So, what do you think of her?

ROOP: I think she is a bit like her dad. Stubborn.

BACHAN (*puzzled*): Who says he is stubborn?

ROOP: She said he is. He brought her here against her wishes. (*He pauses*) She has a strange way of interpreting things.

BACHAN: How so?

ROOP: I showed her that old picture and asked her to look out for that girl. I thought she might come across that girl, so I could see her without Chacha ji finding about it… so I could make up my mind. You know how Mom was putting all that pressure on me.

BACHAN: You did what?

ROOP (*restlessly*): That old picture, Dad. How could I know that it was her?

BACHAN: If you could not recognize her, how did you expect the girl to locate her?

ROOP: Girls have that type of sense. They know things, Dad.

BACHAN: What did she say?

ROOP: She didn't say anything then. Well, she said she would keep an eye out for me. But then she told Chacha ji that I asked her to spy for me. She got upset. How could I know she is the same girl? She was so young. That picture is so faded and she is all grown-up. She thinks I do not have common sense, asking one girl to spy on another. She made me look horrible in Chacha ji's eyes. He must think I am no good. (*He pauses*) And she has a funny way of interpreting things. She refused to see what I was going through.

BACHAN (*sympathetically*): Oh, my boy. You are in deep, deep trouble, up to your eyes. Your mother is angry with you and now this girl is upset. (*He pauses*) You just walked over and gave her the picture?

ROOP (*anxiously*): Oh no, Dad! One day, she was sitting here all bogged down with papers and all that. I thought she was crying…maybe and maybe not, but she did seem very upset. We started talking. She told me how she was brought here against her wishes to study. I felt sorry for her. Then, she asked me.

BACHAN: Asked you what?

ROOP: She asked me what was the matter.

BACHAN: Why?

ROOP: I was sitting there. (*He points toward the chair*) And—

BACHAN: You were just sitting there, and she asked you about what was the matter with you?

ROOP (*exasperated*): Dad, why do you keep interrupting me? I was the one who came over to talk to her when I saw her all bogged down in the papers. And I started talking.

BACHAN: Then?

ROOP: She asked me…why I was looking so gloomy. Maybe I was a little upset…you know how Mom was putting all that pressure on me…I told her how Mom is …oh well, all that stuff.

BACHAN: Just like that, you started to pour your hearts out to each other.

ROOP (*impatiently*): It was not difficult, Father. She can be very nice if she wants to be. It just happened, Dad. I did not plan any of it.

BACHAN: Then, you gave her the picture.

ROOP: Remember Chacha ji was saying his daughter will be joining this university? I thought since both of them are new students, they might run into each other. They may have some classes together.

BACHAN: So, you gave her the picture and asked her to spy for you!

ROOP (*aggravated*): Dad, why do you have to use the word spy?

BACHAN: What else? Why are we sitting here?

ROOP: She may come here in between her classes.

BACHAN: And if she does not?

ROOP (*restlessly*): Why do you have to be so negative, Dad?

BACHAN (*reflectively*): Her father is a very no nonsense type of person. I have known him since childhood. If he gets wind of all this, in addition to your mother's behavior toward them, you won't have a chance with this girl. You better call back the Captain's daughter.

ROOP (*troubled*): Don't say that, Dad. He is your friend. You must convince him. It is not all my fault.

BACHAN: Between you and your mother's games, I will lose a friend, a brother, a part of myself.

ROOP: And he already knows.

BACHAN (*stunned*): He knows?

ROOP: Yes.

BACHAN (*baffled*): How did that happened?

ROOP: Didn't I just mention that she told him?

BACHAN: Oh! Yes, yes, you did.

ROOP (*remorsefully*): Believe me, Dad, it all just happened. I didn't mean for it to happen this way. And I tried to explain it to her, but she does not want to hear a word from me.

BACHAN (*annoyed*): Do you blame her?

ROOP: Chacha ji could have brought her with him to our place. This all would have been avoided. Everything would have been in the open.

BACHAN: In some ways, he is an old-fashioned person. They are staying at her aunt's house. He would not escort his daughter to our house just like that, especially now the way things stand. I may lose my friend, my brother, because of you and your mother!

ROOP (*defensively*): Don't blame this on me, Dad. He has an opinion about everything.

BACHAN: Strong-minded people have strong opinions. At least, you know where they stand. You do not want to be around wishy-washy people who change their minds with every *brolla*[20] of wind.

ROOP: That may be true, but sometimes they rub you wrong way.

BACHAN: Then, that is your problem.

ROOP (*ruefully*): Now, Dad, how is that my problem?

BACHAN: He is an honest and good-hearted man.

ROOP: We are not talking about his heart, Dad. We are talking about his opinions. He has too many.

BACHAN: He says as he sees things.

ROOP (*indignantly*): And, and his daughter... his daughter seems to be just like him.

---

20 ***brolla***. Gust of wind.

BACHAN: You want "yes" people around you. Then, your Chacha ji and his daughter are not your type.

ROOP: It is just like…

BACHAN: He won't say anything just to please you.

ROOP (*distantly*): Dad, sometimes that is all one needs, to hear something just to be pleased. Who does not want that?

BACHAN: More than honesty, integrity, and truthfulness?

ROOP: We are all humans. We need—

BACHAN: He is an open book.

ROOP: Sometimes—

BACHAN: He not only speaks his own mind but also hears and appreciates what you have to say.

ROOP: That may be true, but…

BACHAN: They are simple people, straightforward. They would not stab you in the back. We are simple village folks.

ROOP (*annoyed*): Since when has it become "we"? You want me to—

BACHAN: You do not want people around where you have to weigh every word you say. Where every word you say, every word that comes out of your mouth, is judged. It makes me feel suffocated and dizzy. I can stay there only for a short time.

ROOP: But, Dad!

BACHAN: I like where you can talk openly, you do not have to agree on everything. But there is an underlying good faith. You do not have to prove yourself every time. It is not like walking on glass or thin ice, or as they say here, walking on eggshells. You can be yourself.

ROOP: So, you want me—

BACHAN (*crossly*): No, Son, I do not want to say anything in that regard.

ROOP: But—

BACHAN: No, do not presume anything. You and your mother presume too much.

ROOP: Here she is. Don't turn around. Let me talk to her first.

(*Preet enters. Both of her arms are full of bags and books. She places them on a table near Roop and Bachan, and sits down without noticing them. Roop walks over to her.*)

Roop: Hi.

Preet: Hi! What are you doing here?

Roop (*nervously*): I came to see you.

Preet: See me?

Roop: I want to clear up the misunderstanding.

Preet (*calmly*): There is no misunderstanding.

Roop (*self-consciously*): Chacha ji seemed upset with me.

Preet: Then, talk to him. He and Ranu are moving some of my things in my room. He will be here soon.

Roop: I can help move your things into your dorm room.

Preet: Thank you. My uncle and my father will bring the remaining boxes on Saturday.

Roop: Who is Ranu?

PREET: Some boy in my class. He happened to know my cousin. My father met him when we were leaving the class.

ROOP: Chacha ji went to class with you?

PREET: Oh, no. He was waiting outside. Yesterday, he came with me, just to look around. He said it would give him a sense of my whereabouts during the day. He is a simple but emotional man.

ROOP: He was stubborn, a tyrant, a dictator, and now he is a simple and emotional, too.

PREET: Yes, he is all that and much more.

ROOP: What is left?

PREET: A mother, a grandmother, a brother, and a sister...

ROOP: He is all that?

PREET: He is all that to me.

ROOP: When is he returning home?

PREET: He is leaving on Sunday.

ROOP: This Sunday?

PREET: I will be staying on campus. What would he do? And he needs to take care of the farm.

ROOP: He hasn't returned my dad's phone calls for the past week.

PREET: He hasn't?

ROOP: No.

PREET (*impatiently*): He has lot on his mind. Leaving me here and all that. (*Preet checks her phone*) They are on the way. I would rather leave and meet them outside.

ROOP: Here, let me carry this.

(*Preet collects her scattered bags and books. Roop tries to assist her.*)

PREET: I am all right. It is not far from here.

(*She lets him carry some of the bags.*)

ROOP (*as they are about to leave*): I forgot, my dad came with me to see you. (*He turns to point toward Bachan.*)

PREET: Why didn't you say so earlier? (*She walks over to Bachan. She presses her palms together to greet him.*)

(*Words are exchanged but are not heard by the audience. Bachan exits in haste. They return Preet's belongings to the table.*)

ROOP: I wanted to explain, but...

PREET: There is nothing to explain. I am new here... from the village to boarding school to this new world with new ways. Nobody owes me any explanation.

ROOP: But I do. I must.

PREET (*agitated*): What do you want to say? Say it. I don't hear you saying it. You keep on saying you want to say something, but you don't say anything.

ROOP: Well, I am...I am sorry to drag you into my mess.

PREET: Forget it. It was all in fun. So when will you and the Captain's daughter be hitching up?

ROOP: Hitching up?

PREET: Tying the knot?

ROOP: I don't know. I think they have left.

PREET: They left? Sorry!

ROOP: They might as well.

PREET: Maybe some minister's or other officer's daughter will get lucky. (*She pauses*) I wonder what is taking them so long.

ROOP: Maybe they are trying to get rid of Ranu.

PREET: He has class this evening. Poor boy. He gave my father his phone number. He does not know what he has gotten himself into.

ROOP: To check on you?

PREET: There is no need to check on me. I tell him everything.

ROOP: How could I forget?

PREET: To run my chores, as if I can't do it myself. He can be annoying sometimes.

ROOP: He loves you very much. He is doing all this for you.

PREET (*anxiously looking outside*): What is taking them so long?

ROOP: You don't like the present company?

(*There is a pause.*)

PREET: Here they are.

(*Bachan has a tray, cups, and bags in his hand. Roop pulls two tables together. He serves the coffee.*)

CHACHA JI: The snow looks beautiful. But to walk in it, one needs practice. You can slip and fall without any warning.

PREET (*with concern*): Did you, Father?

CHACHA JI: Don't worry. I did not fall. The sidewalks are all salted. It is cold, very cold. (*He rubs his hands together*) The snow breaks under your boots like *deshi khand*[21] and *ghee*[22] under your teeth.

BACHAN (*looking at Chacha ji's boots*): It is good that you have good winter boots.

CHACHA JI: They do help.

BACHAN: Did you move all of Preet's things in her room?

CHACHA JI: Most of them. (*Addressing Preet*) We set up your room as best as we could. You can rearrange it to

---

21 **desi khand**. Coarse sugar.
22 **ghee**. Clarified butter.

your liking. I like the room. The windows open on the back side, not on the busy street. It is quiet. Just the way you like it.

PREET: Thank you, Father.

CHACHA JI (*to Bachan*): This is a surprise, meeting you here. It is good to see you.

BACHAN: You didn't return my calls.

CHACHA JI: Busy. We have been shopping almost every day, buying all sorts of things for her. It is like setting up a house.

BACHAN (*to Preet*): Didn't you want to stay with your aunt?

CHACHA JI: It was my decision. Her aunt kept insisting that Preet should stay with her. I said let us give it a try. It took us exactly one and a half hours one-way. It would take her three hours just to commute back and forth—to take the bus and then the subway, then classes. Moreover, she is used to staying in hostels.

BACHAN: You remember it used to take us almost an hour to get from our village to school?

CHACHA JI: On our bicycles; in the heat and in the cold.

BACHAN: Those were good days.

ROOP: Bicycle! Chacha ji, I thought you always had that jeep.

CHACHA JI: Not when we were in school.

ROOP: An hour one-way?

CHACHA JI: Yes, and there was no road at that time. (*To Bachan*) Do you remember when it used to rain?

BACHAN: I remember that stretch of path along the bridge; a little bit of rain, and the mud would become as thick as molasses. We used to fall in it every time we got caught in the rain. I still remember every twist and turn on that path, every bush and tree as it used to be before they built the road. Now, it does not feel the same.

CHACHA JI: It is not the same. Before they built the road, they straightened it to avoid sharp turns for the buses and trucks. Remember that water pump? It used to be on the left-hand side on our way to school. Now, it is on the right side…some changes…and the traffic… the peace and quiet of village life is almost gone. But compared to the city, it still feels like a little heaven.

BACHAN: During our last visit, we came very close to selling the land.

ROOP: I can understand how you feel leaving that place. I have visited only a few times, and I feel attached to it.

PREET: And you want me to leave all that and stay here, Father? I don't understand.

CHACHA JI: One day, you will. Your aunt and your cousins are here.

BACHAN: We are here too, daughter! His daughter is my daughter. We are your family, too.

CHACHA JI: I was surprised to see you here. Good surprise.

BACHAN: I could not let you return home without seeing you one more time. You didn't return my calls.

CHACHA JI: I was going to call you tonight. As I mentioned, we were busy collecting things for Preet.

BACHAN: Roop is worried that you are annoyed with him.

CHACHA JI (*to Roop*): Annoyed? Why, my son?

ROOP: I thought you—

CHACHA JI: It is good to leave things as they are. Preet has a good heart and good head on her shoulders. I trust her judgement. She is enrolled in a two-year program. I will be coming back in a few months.

PREET: You will?

CHACHA JI: Of course, I will come to see you!

BACHAN: You are my friend and brother. I can't bear the thought of losing you. It would be like cutting off one of my arms.

CHACHA JI: Don't worry! Let the children sort out their lives. They are good children. Sometimes, it is better to let time run its course.

PREET: Father, let us go and see my room.

ROOP: You have not seen it?

PREET: No. Let us see what Father has done with it.

(*Roop and Preet exit. They wait outside, talking. They are seen but not heard.*)

CHACHA JI: If Preet decides to settle down here, I probably will sell my land.

BACHAN: Don't be hasty.

CHACHA JI: It will ease Preet's burden.

BACHAN: How can it be a burden on her? Don't be childish. Do not sell the land.

CHACHA JI: It will be difficult for her to manage.

BACHAN: Why? Are you planning to renounce the world?

CHACHA JI (*distantly*): Who knows? What is God's will?

BACHAN: You have a long life ahead of you.

(*There is silence.*)

BACHAN: I have not sold my land yet; although, many times I came very close. When money was tight, I was tempted. Many times, I came so close, especially when my parents passed away, even though it is a hassle to manage it from here.

CHACHA JI: I am glad you didn't.

BACHAN: I think both of them will be all right.

CHACHA JI: Both? Who?

BACHAN: Roop and Preet.

CHACHA JI (*calmly but firmly*): I would not agree given Nirmal's disapproval.

BACHAN: She will come around.

CHACHA JI: You know how important it is for the women folk to get along.

BACHAN: Roop is a good boy.

(*Pause.*)

CHACHA JI: Preet is an affectionate and soft-hearted girl. I don't want her to get hurt.

(*Pause.*)

BACHAN: And don't talk foolishly. Selling land! Your daughter is my daughter. She won't be coming into a pauper's house. Nirmal and I have made a life here. We have been working since we came here. So far, with God's grace, Roop has done very well for himself.

CHACHA JI: I leave everything in God's hands. (*He gets up*) As I said, let us see what they decide. I do not want to influence her one way or the other.

BACHAN (*getting up*): Without a doubt. Without a doubt. Whatever they decide. But you must not worry. We are here for her. I am here. You must not worry.

(*Bachan pats Chacha ji's shoulder as they prepare to exit.*)

*Final curtain.*

# VOCABULARY

*aloo-gobbi*. Spicy dish made out of potatoes and cauliflower.

*bai.* Friend, brother.

*beta*. Son

*beti.* Daughter.

*brolla.* Gust of wind.

*burka*. A head to toe dress Muslim women wear to cover themselves.

*Chacha ji.* Father's younger brother in particular or younger male cousin or father's friend.

*deshi khand.* Coarse sugar.

*firangi.* Slang for white foreigner used in India when it was under British rule.

*dal-roti*. *Dal* is a spicy lentil/bean soup. *Roti* is flat bread. The term *dal-roti* is used to mean food in general.

*ghee.* Clarified butter.

**Guru Nanak.** Founder of the religion of Sikhism and is the first of the Sikh Gurus.

**hadd karr ti.** For crying out loud, for God's sake, for goodness's sake.

**janeu or janaeu.** A sacred thread worn by Hindu Brahmins.

**ji.** The term suggests a show of respect.

**langar.** Kitchen.

**LOC.** The term Line of Control (LOC) refers to the military control line between the Indian and Pakistani controlled parts of the state of Jammu and Kashmir.

**massi ji.** Aunt.

**pakoras.** A fried snack made out of chickpea flour, vegetables and spices.

**rehat-mriada.** Way of life.

**sahib.** The term suggests a show of respect.

**sewa.** Charitable service.

***veer ji.*** Brother.

***the wall.*** The two sons of Guru Gobind Singh Ji, Zorawar Singh (nine-years-old) and Fateh Singh (seven-years-old) were bricked up alive within a wall when they refused to convert to Islam. The reference is made to that wall.

# ABOUT THE AUTHOR

H. K. Jeji is a retired high school librarian and teacher. *Crossings* is her first published work. She enjoys travelling, reading and spending time with her family and friends.

www.ingramcontent.com/pod-product-compliance
Lightning Source LLC
Chambersburg PA
CBHW051727040426
42447CB00008B/1017